The Wildlife Pond Handbook

First published in 2003 by New Holland Publishers (UK) Ltd
London • Cape Town • Sydney • Auckland

2 4 6 8 10 9 7 5 3 1

Garfield House, 86-88 Edgware Road, London W2 2EA, United Kingdom
www.newhollandpublishers.com

80 McKenzie Street, Cape Town 8001, South Africa

Level 1/Unit 4, 14 Aquatic Drive, Frenchs Forest, NSW 2086, Australia

218 Lake Road, Northcote, Auckland, New Zealand

All Photography by David M. Cottridge, with the exception of
those listed on page 80
Front cover photograph by Peter Stiles

All artwork commissioned by Wildlife Art Ltd. www.wildlife-art.co.uk,
with the exception of those listed on page 80
Main artists: Robin Carter and Sandra Doyle
Other artist: David Daly

Any prices quoted within the text were up-to-date at time of going to press.

ISBN 1 84330 111 3

Publishing Manager: Jo Hemmings
Project Editor: Lorna Sharrock
Editorial Assistant: Daniela Filippin
Copy Editor: Tim Sharrock
Designer: Alan Marshall
Assistant Designer: Gulen Shevki
Index: Janet Dudley
Production: Joan Woodroffe

Reproduction by Modern Age Repro Co Ltd, Hong Kong
Printed and bound in Malaysia by Times Offset (M) Sdn Bhd

Front cover: Wildlife pond
Back cover: Wildlife pond
Page 1: Common Frog
Page 3: Fringed Water-lily
Page 4: Main photo: Large garden pond; Vignettes: Reeds, Yellow Iris, Wildflowers;
Marsh Marigold; Grey Heron; Water Forget-me-not
Page 5: Main photo: Small garden pond; Vignettes: Common Frog; Banded Demoiselle

THE
wildlife
TRUSTS

The Wildlife Pond Handbook

LOUISE BARDSLEY

**A PRACTICAL GUIDE TO
CREATING AND MAINTAINING YOUR
OWN WETLAND FOR WILDLIFE**

NEW HOLLAND

Contents

The Wildlife Trusts

The Wildlife Trusts partnership is the UK's leading voluntary organization working, since 1912, in all areas of nature conservation. We are fortunate to have the support of more than 366,000 members – many of them are keen gardeners.

We protect wildlife for the future by managing in the region of 2,500 nature reserves, ranging from wetlands and peat bogs, to heaths, coastal habitats, woodlands and wildflower meadows. The Wildlife Trusts works with the general public, planners, businesses, companies and Government to raise awareness of the importance of these threatened habitats and the need to protect them.

The charity also works to influence industry and Government, gives advice to landowners, and runs thousands of activities for adults and children, including Wildlife Watch events.

We encourage people to 'do their bit' for wildlife. We believe that nature conservation can start at home, in our gardens, and a wildlife-friendly pond will support birds, frogs, newts, butterflies, bats, and many other plant and animal species.

With our countryside under increasing threat every garden – big or small – is a potential nature reserve. Gardens also provide a valuable link to parks and other open spaces.

Above: *Tony Blair with Wildlife Trust helpers beside the No. 10 Downing Street wildlife pond.*

Almost one in ten British gardens, including the Prime Minister's residence at No. 10 Downing Street, has a pond. We are working to encourage as many gardeners as possible to ensure theirs are welcoming for wildlife.

Making our 15 million gardens wildlife-friendly will help the plants and animals that make the UK special, and ensure that they are there for future generations to know and enjoy. Being wildlife friendly also means using fewer chemicals, saving gardeners money and helping the environment.

It is amazing just how quickly a mini-wetland area can attract wildlife. Dragonflies and a frog were amongst the first visitors to our show garden at the BBC Gardeners' World Live, at the NEC, within hours of the pond being built!

This book is an invaluable guide to many years of pleasure, and gives you the chance to get close to nature through the seasons.

Thank you for buying The Wildlife Trusts' *The Wildlife Pond Handbook* – we hope you have fun creating and maintaining your very own wetland for wildlife!

The Wildlife Trusts is a registered charity (No. 207238). For membership, and other details, please phone The Wildlife Trusts on 0870 0367711 or log on to www.wildlifetrusts.org

Foreword

There has been a pond in my life for as long as I can remember. Long before I took up water gardening as a career at the age of sixteen, I was already smitten with all things watery – hook, line and sinker, if you will excuse the pun.

During my childhood, our pond gave me endless enjoyment throughout the year. We had goldfish and Golden Orfes in the pond, but that was just the start of it. As the pond matured with the many plants in and around it the wildlife activity fascinated me.

I looked on in wonder at the water boatmen, snails, beetles and skaters. Frogs and toads with their glorious spawn and strings of eggs are wonderful stuff for children to watch. I remember my granddad telling me that frogs and toads nearly always come back to the place they were born to breed themselves. The next year, I waited expectantly for the huge army of metamorphosed tadpoles in the form of toads and frogs to march to our pond. That didn't happen, but we always had plenty of them anyway.

Above: *Fringed Water-lilies provide perfect perches for amphibians and insects as well as great hiding places for small fish.*

The more spectacular visitors to the pond were the beautiful dragonflies and damselflies, which dive bomb you when they first arrive, marking out their territory and behaving as if they were making sure the humans that live around the pond are acceptable. Many birds visited that fed on the insects, including, of course, the heron who soon found the fish. Also, to everyone's initial shock, I saw perfectly harmless Grass Snakes swimming in the water.

I have learnt a lot about ponds and wildlife since those childhood days. What I love about them the most is that you never stop learning. There is always something new and fascinating happening and going on.

Our pond at home turned into a wildlife sanctuary by accident, rather than design, as I am sure many do. So, I was absolutely delighted to be asked to write a foreword for this superb and comprehensive guide to the wildlife pond. It is well overdue and, like ponds themselves, will be a source of inspiration and learning throughout the years.

CHARLIE DIMMOCK

Introduction

Garden ponds are havens for wildlife, welcome islands of tranquillity in our gardens, assets to our homes, laboratories for children, and fun for all the family. The UK has become a nation of pond-lovers since the 1960s, when cheap pond-liners became easily available. Building, restoring and maintaining a wildlife pond are arguably the most useful things that a gardener can do for wildlife.

Right: *Ponds attract wildlife of all shapes and sizes, including the perennial favourite the Mallard. They feed by upending or taking seeds from the surface of the water.*

Ponds may be just a few square metres in area or cover several hectares; they can be deep and hold water all year around, or dry out and hold water for only a few months each year. Some are almost overgrown, whilst others have plants only at their edges. This variety hosts a vast array of wildlife, from flocks of wildfowl and colourful dragonflies to hyperactive whirligig beetles and favourites, such as frogs. As well as being a haven for wildlife, ponds provide a focus for learning about the environment, and can foster a long-term interest in the natural world. The whole web of life can be on display in your garden, and can provide constant entertainment.

The variety of ponds is a joy, but can present problems, since no single management plan will work, and each pond should be maintained individually.

About one-quarter of Britain was covered in wetland (and much of the rest was waterlogged in winter) prior to extensive human influence. Ponds formed in natural dips within the landscape, in river flood plains, and where springs welled up. Sadly, only five per cent of Britain is covered by wetlands today. So, where did all our ponds go?

The simple answer is that they were drained. People have been draining the countryside for agriculture or places to live since before Roman times. Whole tracts have

Right: *Pearls in the landscape – natural ponds should form in hollows of our undrained landscape – if only everywhere was as unspoilt as this Dartmoor pond.*

been drained, such as the creation, in the mid-17th century, of the Bedford Levels, when the Earl of Bedford, using the engineering skills of the Dutchman Sir Cornelius Vermuyden, installed an extensive system of drains and diverted the Old Bedford and the Great Ouse Rivers. As a result of this huge drainage scheme, the peat shrank, creating a drop in land level across the Fens, so that water now has to be pumped uphill.

Even a small drop in water level can dry out small water-bodies, such as ponds, pools and lakes, so that seasonal pools are now a rare and precious habitat. Many lowland rivers have been straightened, widened and deepened, so that the natural meanders that would eventually have become new ponds no longer exist. Flood-defences, created to protect buildings on the flood plain, constrain water flow and prevent the natural overflowing of rivers.

With all this drainage, has our countryside become devoid of all pond life? Fortunately not!

Man-made ponds

Along with drastic land drainage, ponds have been created, also for agricultural reasons. In an earlier age, every farm and village would have had a pond to provide water for livestock, for horses and for irrigating crops. Some were stocked with fish and others were used for boating, skating or bathing. There are a variety of different ponds that remain today, some of which are detailed below.

Hilltop dewponds can be found throughout downland in southern England and in the limestone hills of Derbyshire and east Yorkshire. The many names of these ponds imply mysterious origins, including fog, mist or cloud ponds. In reality they were created by farmers, during the

Above: *Village ponds were a vital part of the rural economy until the late 19th century. Many still remain and with a little help from an enthusiastic local community village ponds could be teeming with wildlife.*

Above: *Ornamental ponds like this one can be great for wildlife, if they are not over-stocked with fish. Watch out for those water-lilies, as they tend to take over smaller ponds.*

19th and early 20th century, to provide water for livestock. These artificial ponds often lie neglected, but some are still used in the traditional way by local people.

Freshwater fish have been harvested from stocked and specially maintained fish ponds since before the Middle Ages. These fishponds were often deep (up to 3m) and dish-shaped, lined with clay, timber or wattle, and were protected from animals and human poachers by walls or fences. Today, few remain, but examples can be seen at older abbeys, such as Denny Abbey and Anglesey Abbey, both in Cambridgeshire.

Historically, many areas of fen, bog and wetland were cut by hand to provide peat to be used as fuel. These small-scale cuttings did not completely destroy the wetlands, and often created habitat suitable for wildlife. One example of this is the large, shallow lakes of the Norfolk Broads, which were created mainly by peat cutting in the 12th to 15th centuries.

Modern peat cutting is an entirely different affair. Large-scale commercial cutting, using mechanical peat-cutters, is more likely to destroy a wetland completely than to create small ponds and lakes.

Wildfowl such as ducks were an important source of food in the 16th to 18th centuries. Large, shallow lakes were adapted or constructed, with ditches leading off them, called pipes, below tunnels of netting. Ducks were attracted to these duck decoy ponds and then lured into the pipes, where they were caught for food. These decoy ponds were at their heyday in the 17th and 18th centuries, but, sadly, most have been filled in or simply neglected. The last working decoy pond is probably that at Abbotsbury, Dorset, where the birds are caught, ringed and released, not killed for food.

Ponds for more industrial purposes have been created since Saxon times. Holding lakes were constructed to retain water to feed through a channel, or leat, to the waterwheels that powered mills. The production of rope, cord and hemp, and the curing of animal skins, all required water supplies. As industry developed further in the 17th to 19th centuries, clay was dug for brick-making and ceramics, and marl extracted from the soil as a fertiliser.

More recently, lakes and ponds have been created as ornamental features in retail and business parks as well as to provide challenges for golfers. Gravel pits are found all over the UK, mainly in river valley flood plains. Small abandoned pits often flood, forming miniature wetlands. Unless in-filled and restored as dry land, many large excavations are deliberately flooded for recreation, such as boating, water-skiing or fishing and for conservation purposes, such as keeping wildfowl.

The modern garden pond has a long and rather grand history. Having an ornamental lake that could be viewed from the house became a fashion on country estates in the 18th and 19th centuries. Landscape gardeners, such as Joseph Paxton, created enormous feats of engineering, such as the Canal Pond at Chatsworth House. The garden ponds of the 21st century are usually constructed on a much-less-grand scale, but now constitute about one-fifth of all the shallow pond habitat in England and Wales.

This variety of man-made ponds do not, however, wholly compensate for the natural pools that have been lost, since they tend to be deeper, to have steeper sides, to have permanent water, and to be isolated from other water-bodies. Wildlife that lives in ponds needs gentle slopes to enter and leave the water.

The 21st-century pond

By the end of the 20th century, over three-quarters of the ponds that dotted our countryside at the start of the century had been lost, as their traditional uses became redundant. Even today, when their value is known, ponds are still being destroyed at a rate of about one per cent per year.

Natural ponds and wetlands usually form a mosaic, with pools of different depths and sizes, some of which may dry out in summer, but which may all link up in winter. This mosaic of ponds allows plants and animals that may die out in one area to re-colonize, in a natural cycle. Isolation makes this impossible, or very much less likely.

The small size and static water of ponds makes them vulnerable to pollution. On arable

land, streams and ditches running through agricultural fields can pick up nutrients, silt and pesticides, which then accumulate in the pond. Ponds can be buffered from the worst effects of farming by leaving unploughed strips alongside streams, ditches and ponds. Polluted ponds can be restored relatively easily and cheaply. The long-term solution is sustainable farming, with grazing pressure, fertilizer use and pesticide input all reduced.

Well-meaning, inadvertent mismanagement is another threat to ponds. Shallow, temporary ponds may be deepened in an attempt to prevent them from drying out, or ponds which have become overgrown by vegetation are cleared out, thereby not only destroying the plants, but also killing the animals that had colonized the pond. Garden ponds are often mismanaged for wildlife by people who do not have access to the correct information. The main aim of this book is to remedy that.

Above: *To many people this pond looks completely overgrown, but it could be harbouring rare beetles or unusual species of rush.*

Planning a Pond

When you are planning a new wildlife pond, a visit to a nearby wild pond is bound to provide you with inspiration. The range of animals that you can attract to your pond, and the plants and creatures that will live happily in it, will be influenced by where you live and how far the nearest pond is.

A pond in the heart of a big city in lowland England will be different from one in a village in the Scottish Highlands. How close your pond is to other wetlands will also affect what is likely to reach your pond and what can survive and thrive in it.

To help you locate your nearest wildlife ponds, it may be helpful to peruse the relevant Ordnance Survey map, do some research on the Internet or make enquiries at your local Wildlife Trust. A visit to a wild pond will reveal the range of animals and plants that occurs naturally in your area. You may also be able to work out how far your garden is from the nearest pond, and the likelihood that aquatic plants and animals will spread naturally. Don't be put off if there is no other pond nearby: that just makes it all the more important that you create your own wildlife oasis in the local urban or rural desert.

Right: A large pond like this one takes a lot of planning, but isn't it worth it? The variety of plant and animal species that will flourish in a large pond make your hard work worthwhile.

Once you have located a suitable pond, draw a simple sketch, or take a few photographs, as reminders to help you to plan your pond when you get back home.

Take a note of the plant mixtures and how much (or how little) water is open with no vegetation. Do not worry about identifying every plant species, though this can be fun if you have a good field guide; just observe that the tall vegetation at the edge of the pond changes to shorter, stockier plants and finally to those with floating leaves. Look underwater to see any submerged plants.

Note the different shapes of plant, where they are grouped, and the range of colours, from the subtle greens and browns of rushes to spectacular Yellow Iris or the delicate blues of Water Forget-me-not. (Be careful: do not stand where you are unsure of the depth of water or the firmness of the ground. Follow the safety advice at the back of this book (*Health and safety* on page 75), and remember: *if in doubt, don't do it!*)

Loved ones and the law

Armed with your sketches and photographs of natural ponds, you may feel ready to begin planning your own garden pond for wildlife. It is best to take a while to consider other garden users. There is no point in building a beautiful pond if the children will trample the wetland-meadow edges or puncture the lining in pursuit of their football or tennis ball.

It is a good idea to sit down with everyone who uses the garden and discuss your plans. If you are really lucky, you may even get help to plan, build and look after the pond. It is also worth having a chat with your neighbours, especially if the pond you are considering building is of lake-like proportions.

Left: *Common is not always a bad thing. Water Forget-me-not is one of the UK's commonest waterside plants – and what a gem. With its gentle blue flowers this will grace any garden pond.*

Left: *Who said native plants are dull? Yellow Iris is one of the easiest plants to establish around the edge of your wetland and it looks great, flowering from May to August.*

Above: *We can't all produce sketches like this one, but taking a photograph and a few notes of your local natural ponds will give you inspiration for your own garden pond.*

Most garden ponds will not require any sort of formal planning permission, but it is wise to telephone your local planning authority to check. Planning permission will, however, be required for any pond built on land that is not privately owned. If you plan to dig a pond within the flood plain, you will need to contact the Environment Agency (in England and Wales), the Scottish Environmental Protection Agency (in Scotland) or the Environmental Heritage Services (in Northern Ireland).

If you wish to take water from a main river, you should consult the relevant environment agency or landowner. You may require a special water-removal licence (an 'abstraction licence'); if you wish the water to flow back from your pond into the river, you may require an additional licence (a 'discharge licence/consent'). Trees may have Tree Preservation Orders on them, and the whopping £20,000 fine (per tree!) imposed in some areas makes prior investigation essential before carrying out any tree surgery.

MOVING PLANTS AND ANIMALS – THE LAW

Many aquatic animals harbour diseases or parasites, and non-native plants often hitchhike on native plants. Take care not to transfer disease or non-native plants from one pond to another.

It can be difficult to obtain native wetland plant species from garden centres, and many aquatic specialists stock mainly exotics. This does not, however, mean that you should dig up plants from your nearest wild pond: this is against the law. Uprooting wild plants is an offence under the Wildlife and Countryside Act, 1981. It is also theft, if you take them, without permission, from privately-owned land.

As a guideline: **NEVER REMOVE PLANTS OR ANIMALS FROM THE WILD.**

There are several laws that protect wildlife and the environment in the UK, most of which do not apply directly to privately owned gardens. Species protected under the Wildlife and Countryside Act, 1981, however,

Above: *Great Crested Newts are legally protected, so look but don't touch.*

and those given additional protection under the Countryside and Rights of Way Act, 2000, are usually still legally protected, even if they are in a garden.

The most widespread legally-protected species likely to be found in or around a garden pond are bats, Great Crested Newts and Water Voles. To capture or handle these species, even if you are trying to count or protect them, you must obtain a licence from a conservation agency (see pages 76–7). If you want to translocate fish, contact the relevant environment agency. If you want to move something into a pond where a protected species is already present, you must consult a conservation agency. Also, seek advice from your local Wildlife Trust.

To make sure that you stay within the law, simply propagate plants from a friend's pond. Do not stock any animals in your pond: just let them find their way on their own. This may take a year or so, but it will be worth the wait.

Getting to know your garden

So, your family has agreed, the planning authority has been consulted, and your neighbours think it's a great idea. Surely the next thing is to get your spade and wellies out? Well, no. There are no unbreakable rules, but, to give yourself the best possible pond, you need to do a little bit more planning and a little investigation.

The aspect of your garden (whether it faces north, south, east or west) will affect where and when the sun shines on your pond. Trees, shrubs, walls and other structures will all create shaded water, which is cooler than that in full sunlight, and the water temperature affects the wildlife in your pond. The ideal is for part, but not all, of your garden pond to be in full sunlight. If your garden is south facing and there is little or no natural shade, part of the pond could be shaded by a trellis or by judicious planting. In a very shady garden, you may need to prune a few trees or bushes to let in more light.

Siting a pond under a tree seems like a great idea, but if the pond is small and the tree is large it will not only shade the whole pond, but also fill it with leaves. Some leaf litter can be a good thing, and large ponds and lakes may benefit from being partially shaded by trees: many insect species (known as detritivores) feed on dead, decaying leaves and wood.

As with all things, however, it is important to try to achieve a balance, between sun and shade. Another disadvantage of siting a pond close to a tree is that digging may disturb its root system, which could make the tree unstable. The roots will continue to grow after the pond is constructed and may penetrate the pond-lining, causing a leak. If possible, therefore, it is best to site your pond a little away from trees and tall shrubs.

If your garden is very exposed to the prevailing wind, it is wise to site your pond on the lee side of trees, tall shrubs or a trellis. By doing this you will give some shelter from the wind and, if it is a large pond, stop wave action from eroding the soil on the windward side.

Above: *Large ponds like this one can cope with shade on one side, but too much shade will reduce pond plant growth. Also, shade may stop some invertebrates from visiting your pond.*

Right: *This is a fantastic pond, but it would not succeed without good quality water and plenty of it. When planning your pond and deciding its size, consider your water source carefully.*

A great way of keeping your pond full of water is to site your pond at the bottom of a slope as it will collect water naturally. You will need to level the edges of the slope before digging your pond. Water running straight into a pond across bare soil will pick up silt and nutrients, which can lead to problems with silting up and algal blooms. A border of vegetation, such as long grasses or a bog garden, will help to avoid such problems.

The type of soil in your garden will affect the way that water drains or does not drain. If there is underlying clay, you may be able to create a pond in the ground without lining it. In most instances, however, you will need to line your pond. For stony soils, the one-off effort of removing stones may be tedious, but will pre-empt a lot of management problems later.

What water?

The most important part of a pond is its water. Just as soil acidity or alkalinity (its pH) and nutrients affect the plants in your garden, so they also affect what animals can live in your pond. You can test the pH of your water quite easily, using strips that can be purchased from most aquarium specialists and garden centres.

Nutrients occur in the silt within a pond, and accumulate from the decomposition of dead plants and animals. Algae can grow in such vast quantities in water rich in nutrients that ponds can become choked and the water can appear bright green. Choosing a water source with low nutrients is preferable to trying to remove them. Water is so important to your pond's health that it is worth considering the ways that a pond can be filled with water.

The surface water that runs off the soil, or over patios and concreted or tarmacked areas, will fill a pond, especially if it is positioned at the bottom of a slope.

Groundwater, held in rocks and sediments below the soil, feeds many natural wetlands, often in the form of springs. This naturally-filtered water is usually low in nutrients and free of most pollutants, and is the best water supply for a pond. It is, however, unusual for garden ponds to be groundwater fed, as houses are seldom built in areas of high groundwater because of the risk of flooding.

Many ponds on agricultural land are linked to drainage pipes or ditches that feed water from the surrounding land into the pond. The water quality in drainage channels and inflows depends on the use of the drained land. A pond

fed with high-nutrient water from agricultural land will be susceptible to algal blooms and to rapid silting up.

It may be possible to create a pond using water fed from a nearby stream. You could create a pool by damming the flow, or a side channel could be dug to divert water to your pond. Such ponds require careful planning, and may require licences (see *Loved ones and the law* on pages 13–14). If you are creating a pond with major water flows, it is probably best to consult a specialist firm or a hydrologist.

The water quality in a stream-fed pond will be influenced by the quality of the stream water. In lowland England, the water will often be rich in nutrients and silt, leading to the problems mentioned previously. Smaller streams, especially those on higher ground in hills and mountains, are less likely to be polluted, and a constant flow of water maintains the high oxygen levels required by many invertebrates and fish species. Stream-fed ponds can also be very rich in wildlife, as the stream provides a rapid and constant source of new species.

All this being said, most small garden ponds are built with a pond-liner and then filled with tap water. The main disadvantage to this is that tap water contains additives, including chlorine. Fortunately, it loses its chlorine if left to stand for a few days – the chlorine degrades down to something much less harmful to wildlife.

Tap water may also contain nutrients, especially nitrates, and these can lead to excessive algal or plant growth. The best way to fill your pond is with rainwater. Use a water butt to collect the rainwater from your roof.

Designing a Pond

There is a myth that bigger is better: some people believe that there is more wildlife in lakes and rivers than in small ponds. When surveyed carefully, however, it was found that a sample of 150 ponds had slightly more invertebrate species than did a sample of 600 rivers and streams. The ponds also had many more rare species.

One large lake will probably have more species living in it than one small pond, but several small ponds will have more species than one large lake covering the same area. The rule is simple: diversity of habitat leads to diversity of species living within an area.

With water depth, the same is true: a range of ponds of different depths offers variety for a range of species. Most aquatic invertebrates live in very shallow water (less than 30cm) and many more plants grow in the shallow margins and damp wetlands around ponds than are found in the deeper, open water.

If you have space for a large lake, it is worth considering an alternative, and far-more-interesting option: a series of small ponds of differing depths, designed to interlink in winter and allowed to dry out a little in summer. If some are occasionally allowed to dry out altogether, this will benefit species that habitually use temporary ponds. Rare species like the Fairy Shrimp (*Chirocephalus diaphanous*) and Tadpole Shrimp (*Triops cancriformis*), as well as several water beetles, are all specialists of temporary ponds and water bodies.

If you have the time and resources to build only a single pond, then make it as large as possible. Maximize the diversity within it by varying the profile (height and steepness of the slopes).

When planning your wildlife pond, the outline is entirely up to you. In profile, however, it should have gently sloping sides, which are not only safer for children, but also make access and egress easy for animals of all sizes. The shallow water on the slopes will provide good habitat for marsh plants, and consequently for many invertebrates such as dragonflies. Water expands when it freezes, and a steep-sided pond lined with a solid material such as concrete could be cracked by expanding ice.

It is best to try to mimic natural pond shapes; stark geometric shapes can look out of place, except in a formal garden, and are difficult to line. Make allowance for over-spill of the pond in very rainy weather. The creation of a bog garden or marshy area can take advantage of this.

Position perfect

After checking the distribution and position of trees and shade in your garden (see *Getting to know your garden* on page 15), decide where you could best enjoy your pond. You may want to see the pond from your house, perhaps from the kitchen window or the sitting room, or have it beside a seating or patio area. Alternatively, in a large garden, you may wish to site the pond away from the house, in a more-secluded, peaceful area, where shy species are more likely to visit. You will certainly want to have easy access for maintenance, and also for watching wildlife at close quarters. You will probably need to top up the water level from time to time, so check that your hosepipe will reach the planned pond area.

Obviously, you need to ensure that the pond is not sited near drains or cables that could be damaged or which might need to be inspected or replaced. If your garden is already well established, it may be best to avoid siting it in any existing wetland, which could be home to important species. If in doubt, ask for advice from your local Wildlife Trust.

Choosing a lining

Urban areas are often well drained and garden ponds almost invariably have to be lined to hold water. Dewponds were lined with clay and 'clay puddling' is still used today, although it is difficult to work with, requires large amounts of clay, and is expensive. For this reason, most small gardens did not have ponds until the advent of cheap synthetic liners in the 1960s.

All linings need to be ultraviolet-resistant and non-biodegradable, or they will break down when exposed to sunlight and air. Of course, the most important property of a pond-liner is that it is completely waterproof.

There are many different types and qualities of lining, but a rough guide is that the more that you spend the longer the pond will last. The *Pond-liners* table on page 21 provides a quick reference for comparison of the costs, durability, advantages and disadvantages of different materials and types.

If your pond is accessible to the public (for example, in your front garden) it will also be vulnerable to vandalism, or may present a danger to children. Options to consider to prevent damage to an accessible pond include putting up a fence, or having a layer of dense vegetation around your pond.

Opposite: *Planting low-growing vegetation nearer the house allows you to view the pond and larger, taller plants at the back will add perspective. It is best to create a variety of habitats for wildlife.*

Below: *Mixing different types of pond plants together not only provides interest to your garden but also provides habitat for beetles, bugs, birds, bees and more besides.*

Puddled clay

Puddled clay is a traditional lining for ponds. Clay is cut and laid like paving, the lumps being abutted as tightly as possible, and then watered and 'puddled'. Puddling is done by trampling the joins to form a continuous layer of wet sticky clay. Traditionally, this was done by driving cattle or sheep repeatedly over the wet clay. If you are creating a very large pond and do not have a handy flock of sheep, puddling can be carried out by using a rubber-tracked vehicle.

It is difficult and tiring to puddle a small pond by hand, but a clay lining can produce a very natural-looking, easily planted pond. As the water level drops, clay can dry out and crack, so such ponds need to be kept wet right up to the top of the lining. Cracks can be mended by adding wetted clay or bentonite, but this is not always easy. Clay can be purchased already puddled or wetted, but it is heavy, so transportation is expensive.

Bentonite

Bentonite is a naturally occurring non-toxic clay that, when wetted, swells to ten to 20 times its dry volume. Powdered bentonite can be quite difficult to use as a liner, but it is useful for repairing leaks. For small garden ponds, it can be easier to use Geosynthetic Clay Liner (GCL).

Below: *Once a wildlife pond is well established, which takes about a year, the lining should no longer be visible. Planting a variety of plant species around the edges will speed this process.*

POND-LINERS

A quick reference guide to the perfect liner for your pond.

Lining type	Price per square metre	Notes
Butyl flexible liner	£4.50 – £5.50	Easy to fit, stretches, and is long lasting (>20 years). UV-resistant and has a range of grade sizes suitable for different uses and pond types.
Clay puddling	Variable: depends on type of clay (wet or dry) and transport costs.	Difficult to install, and vulnerable to crack ing, but can last a lifetime (>50 years). Very expensive.
Concrete	£10 – £15	Difficult to install, and vulnerable to crack ing, but can last a lifetime (>50 years).
EPDM rubber (Ethylene Propylene Diene Monomer) 45mm for garden ponds; 60mm for school or public-access ponds	£5.50 – £8.00	Easy to fit, since it stretches. Similar to Butyl, but with longer life-span (>30 years, even in full sunlight).
Geotextile Clay Liner (GCL) (raw mat)	£6.00	Can be difficult to install and is prone to punctures, but relatively easy to repair.
Heavy-duty polythene 1000–2000 gauge	£1.00 – £3.00	Relatively short-lived (5–10 years) and prone to both puncture and splitting. Very difficult to repair.
Polyester protective matting (at least 3mm thick)	£0.85 – £3.00	Can be used as protection from punctures when using one of the other liners. Better than carpet, as it will not rot. Thick layer of sand can be used instead, but will be more prone to movement and settling.
Polyethylene (LDPE)	£5.00 – £3.50	UV-stabilised plastic liner. Less prone to cracking and splitting than polythene, since it stretches, making it easy to fit. Should last for about 20 years, and possibly longer.
Pre-cast liners made from fibreglass or plastic	£10.30 approx.	Can be difficult to fit, since they are not flexible and their pre-cast shape limits their potential. Prone to cracking and difficult to repair, but have a relatively long life span (> 20 years).
PVC	£1.60 – £2.20	Stretches and is relatively easy to fit. Long life expectancy (15–25 years).

Above: *Flexible pond-liners revolutionized pond creation. Now, every garden can have a wet wildlife haven. Most synthetic liners look similar, but have different applications. Shown here are, from left to right, PVC, butyl rubber and heavy duty rubber.*

Above: *This pond may look untidy to some gardeners, but not to me and not to wildlife. By having plenty of dead wood you will attract insects and other invertebrates, and marginal plants help dragonflies to clamber out of the water.*

GCL is a sandwich of bentonite clay between two layers of woven material known as geotextile. The bentonite within these liners is wetted under pressure, making the combination less likely to dry out and to crack. GCLs are flexible and easy to use. Joining adjacent sections is simple: overlapped edges join when wetted. This material is particularly suited to wildlife ponds, since root growth does not cause leakage. GCLs can be shaped against other materials, so are suitable even where a vertical edge is required. Bentonite does not, however, always work well on sandy or other non-clay substrates, since it may not bond chemically with the surrounding soils. It can also clog the gills of fish if they are put into the pond too soon after construction.

Concrete
Concrete-lined ponds are difficult to construct. Concrete linings are poured into constructed moulds, which are usually geometric shapes, so look unnatural. Unless the pond is very large, creating the shallow gradients required for a wildlife pond may be impossible. Concrete linings are probably best left to specialist contractors. Since the lining is inflexible, it may crack, especially when water freezes and expands. The soil below a concrete-lined pond needs to be very thoroughly compacted prior to construction, to prevent subsidence and cracking.

Synthetic liners
Pre-cast plastic liners are not ideal for wildlife ponds, since their sides are usually too steep, planting wetland edge plants is impracticable, and their pre-formed shapes may not suit the chosen site.

For most garden ponds, flexible synthetic liners are best, as these are relatively cheap and easy to use. Using a little thought and planning, a very natural-looking pond can be created.

Many different types of synthetic liner are available, but all eventually break down with age and exposure to sunlight. Polythene and PVC liners are difficult to repair and the most effective remedy is often to start again, relining the leaking pond.

The most user-friendly flexible lining for garden ponds are butyl liners. Liners are sold by the metre from rolls of different widths. Specialist stockists will have rolls up to 8m or even 10m wide. For very large ponds or lakes, which are wider than the maximum roll width, liners can be welded together on site, but this requires professional expertise, which will obviously add to the cost of your pond.

Filters, pumps and chemicals

There are a huge number of devices available for your pond, ranging from filters that sieve out everything larger than a few microns to UV filters that zap the water with intense UV-light, killing not only all the algae, but also all the small animal life that lives in a pond. Pumps are required to push the water through the filters, and to oxygenate it. There are chemicals that kill all the algae and claim to give you clean and clear water. They do indeed create clean water, but only because there is nothing living in it. These products are aimed mainly at the ornamental-fish-pond owner, who wants to see his or her beautiful Koi Carp swimming in crystal-clear water.

Such ponds are often designed to have a huge number of fish that cannot possibly be supported by the food naturally available in their pond. They therefore require artificial food, which adds large amounts of nutrients to the pond, as does the excreta from the fish. These nutrients favour the growth of algae, and the filters and pumps have killed everything that would eat the algae. As a result, more filters or chemicals are needed to stop the water going green, so there are then even more free nutrients ... I think you can see the pattern that is forming. These products also cost a fortune, with some more-complicated, integrated systems costing hundreds of pounds.

A wildlife pond will achieve the right balance between algae, grazing animals and predators naturally. Nature provides its own filters (water fleas (see page 58)) and its own oxygenators (plants). So long as a pond does not have too many nutrients or too many fish, it will have clear water and enough oxygen. A few small, native fish, such as sticklebacks, are very appropriate in a small pond, and large ponds can even accommodate a few of the bigger species. Large numbers of ornamental fish are, however, not appropriate in a wildlife pond. If you want to keep fish, build them a fishpond, and you may even be lucky and get a little wildlife in it. If you want a wildlife pond, leave the fish to someone else, or get yourself an indoor aquarium.

Above: *Koi Carp are spectacular, but they are not really compatible with a wildlife pond. If you love these fish, build them their own pond and build a separate one for wildlife.*

Building a Wildlife Pond

Once you have checked with the planning authority and other garden users for permission to create your aquatic masterpiece, you have a suitable design and location and plenty of water available, you are ready to start building your pond.

EQUIPMENT

- Wellies and outdoor clothes
- Stakes
- Rope/string
- Non-toxic biodegradable spray paint
- Spade or mini-digger
- Fork
- Buckets/wheel-barrow
- Board
- Spirit level
- Protective matting/soft sand
- Liner
- Large stones
- Hosepipe

Below: *A fibrous synthetic underlay helps protect the liner from sharp stones and roots.*

Building small ponds

Making a small, lined garden pond (length 1–5m) is a ten-step process, the first nine steps of which can be accomplished within one week.

1 Marking out the shape

To create a perfect circle, place a stake in the middle of your area, attach a rope to it, hold the rope taut and walk around the stake, spraying the ground with non-toxic, biodegradable spray paint as you go. Natural ponds are, however, rarely perfectly circular; so outlining a series of smaller circles to form bays around your main circle will create a more natural shape. Alternatively, use a piece of rope or old hosepipe to mark out an irregular shape.

This is also the time to determine the lowest point outside the pond area to position your wetland or bog garden. This will ensure that your bog garden is the wettest area at the edge of your pond.

Once you have marked out the shapes on the ground, look at them from all the places from which you plan to view the finished pond, and also from a high vantage point, such as an upstairs window. If the shape is not quite what you want, redraw it on the ground.

2 Excavating

Next, dig the hole. If the area is covered in grass, cut the turf into squares, roll up and stack in piles to be used later to edge the pond.

Keep the nutrient-rich topsoil and more stony subsoil separate, as you will want to use them for different purposes later. Surplus topsoil can be used to create a sloping bank away from the pond, to landscape the rest of your garden, to create a raised bed, or to fill patio containers. When using a spade, it is simplest to dig out small sections at a time, to form a roughly square shape, and to create the smooth curves and edges later. For slightly larger ponds, it may be worth hiring a mini-digger, to save both time and your back. When operating machinery, ensure that children are out of harm's way, follow safety instructions, and avoid digging up a cable or sewer pipe.

The edges of a pond should slope gently. If the pond is small and requires a deep centre, it is possible to create a gently sloping shelf at the edge, with a second, steeper slope into the middle. For slightly larger ponds, a series of undulations will help to create a variety of depths. Most of the pond should be less than 50cm deep with a deeper central channel.

3 Checking shape and level

Once you have the approximate shape, make sure that the outside edges are roughly at the same height. For very small ponds, this can be done by placing a board across the edges and using a spirit level. For larger areas, you can put pegs around the edge of the pond and use a board to check the level between each peg.

4 Preparing the base

Once the shape is dug out, the ground can be prepared by picking over the top few centimetres and removing any stones, roots and debris that might damage the pond-liner. For additional protection, line the hole with protective matting or soft sand. A cheap alternative is old newspapers, but beware of staples. Newspapers will eventually rot, possibly causing subsidence and could lead to the liner leaking.

Excavating and shaping your pond

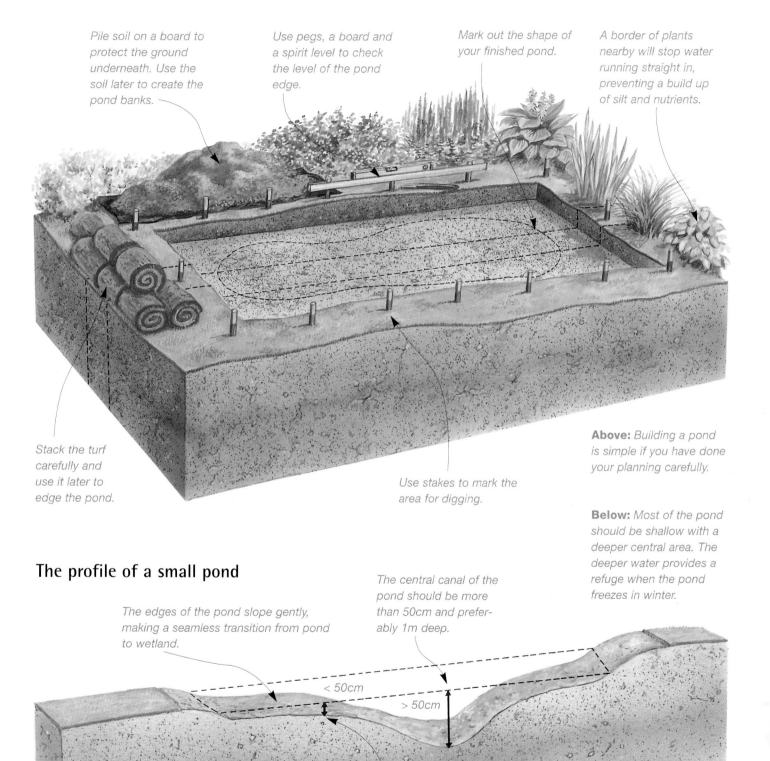

Pile soil on a board to protect the ground underneath. Use the soil later to create the pond banks.

Use pegs, a board and a spirit level to check the level of the pond edge.

Mark out the shape of your finished pond.

A border of plants nearby will stop water running straight in, preventing a build up of silt and nutrients.

Stack the turf carefully and use it later to edge the pond.

Use stakes to mark the area for digging.

Above: *Building a pond is simple if you have done your planning carefully.*

Below: *Most of the pond should be shallow with a deeper central area. The deeper water provides a refuge when the pond freezes in winter.*

The profile of a small pond

The edges of the pond slope gently, making a seamless transition from pond to wetland.

The central canal of the pond should be more than 50cm and preferably 1m deep.

< 50cm

> 50cm

The majority of the pond should be less than 50cm deep to provide plenty of shallow water for marginal plants and the invertebrates that live there.

Another option to keep the liner taut is to fill the pond with water before adding the subsoil. The weight of the water will ensure the liner is tight to the sides. Then siphon off the water and continue with step 6.

5 Measuring and positioning the liner
Deciding how much liner is needed requires a fairly simple calculation. The total width needed is the width of the pond plus twice the depth of the pond. The total length of liner needed is the length of the pond plus twice the depth of the pond. For a pond that is 3m maximum width, 5m maximum length and has a maximum depth of 0.5m the liner would need to be:

3m + (2 x 0.5)m wide by 5m + (2 x 0.5)m long.

Thus, you would require a liner at least 4m wide by 6m long. If you are creating a wetland or bog garden at the edge of the pond, this will need to be included in your calculations, since the bog garden will need to be lined.

Lay the liner over the pond and put subsoil into the centre (coarsely sieved to remove all sharp stones and roots that could puncture it). The weight of the soil will keep the liner taut.

6 Adding subsoil for rooted plants
The liner can then be covered with a 2–3cm layer of subsoil (it will contain less nutrients than topsoil). The edges of the liner should be dug in or held in place by large rounded stones or soil.

Towards the edges of the pond, increase the soil depth, particularly in the area of the bog garden or wetland. If the pond is very small, you may wish to add topsoil only at the edges, and use baskets for deep-water plants.

Measuring the liner

Right: *To get the width of liner you need add the width of the pond to twice the depth = W + 2D.
To get the length of liner you need add the length of the pond to twice the depth = L + 2D.*

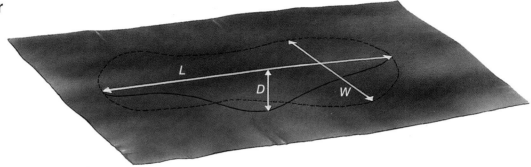

Lining and planting your pond

Right: *Once the pond is lined you can add the plants. The shape of the pond will create areas for different types of plants including wetland and floating plants.*

Hold down the edge of the lining with stones to ensure it stays in position.

The shallow margins are ideal for tall emergent plants, such as Lesser Reed Mace.

Floating-leaved and submerged plants grow in the deeper parts of the pond.

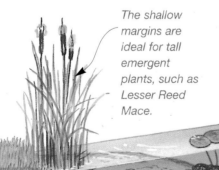

Line the edge of the pond and underneath the wetland. The soil depth here can be as much as 10cm deep.

Use baskets to restrict the growth of very vigorous plants such as lilies.

The shallow slope at the edge creates room for lots of rooted plants. Plant both low-growing and tall species.

7 Adding water
Slowly add a little water and leave it to settle for one or two days. Tap water can be run into the pond from a hosepipe laid into the deepest part of the pond. Filling your pond from rainwater in a water butt is an even better option (see *What Water?* on page 16).

8 Adding plants
Small garden ponds should not be planted until about one week after they have been filled, to allow silt to settle to the bottom of the pond and the water to clear. This will also allow you to check for any leaks or minor adjustments prior to planting. Plant your wetland or bog garden at the same time as the pond.

9 Reviewing what has been achieved
When the pond is mostly planted, take time to review your plans. You may want to adjust the position of some plants or to add more topsoil to the edges, the wetland or the bog garden.

10 Making wildlife-friendly borders
Once the pond is planted, the rest of your garden can be made more wildlife friendly by creating a rockery, adding piles of dead wood or perhaps creating a wildflower meadow. Putting up bird and bat boxes and putting out food will attract more creatures. *Fantastic Features* on page 32 describes simple, effective measures that anyone can take to make a garden literally buzz with wildlife.

Below: *This mature garden has lots of interest for wildlife; the tall trees provide birds with perches and the dense bushes are great for nesting birds. Remember, variety is the spice of life!*

Building large ponds

Building a large pond (length >5m) or a series of interlinking small ponds requires considerably more detailed planning than does the construction of a single small pond. All the initial stages, such as checking for water sources and finding the ideal position, are the same, but a large pond may require additional permission and licences. Check with the relevant environment agency that there will be enough water to fill your pond.

Listed below are the stages in the creation of a series of small clay-lined ponds that will join up in winter to form a large lake. This will provide a wide variety of habitats and will attract a good cross section of wildlife. The construction method will, however, work only if the soil is clay that can be used as a lining.

building work, get the work plan, exact specifications and timescale agreed. Ensure that the contract is for a fixed price, so that if the contractor makes a mistake and goes over budget it is not you who has to pay.

Consulting both the appropriate conservation and environmental agencies will help to establish your legal position. You may need a licence to build an embankment or to dispose of large amounts of waste soil. Waste disposal is very expensive, so it is much better to use surplus soil to create landscape features elsewhere. This should be agreed with the contractor at the outset. As with small ponds, licences may be required if you are taking water from or discharging water into a stream or river, or if the pond is within 7m of a riverbank. Stocking your lake with fish may also require a licence.

EQUIPMENT/ SPECIALISTS

- Specialist contractors
- Sketches of design
- Hydraulic excavator (digger) and driver
- Outdoor clothing
- Theodolite

Below: Larger ponds offer more scope for interesting and varied design. Create lots of little pools designed to join together in winter (compare to page 30).

1 Choosing an expert and seeking advice
Unless you are a qualified hydraulic-excavator driver, you will need to employ a specialist contractor who will not only dig a hole, but will also oversee the survey and construction of the pond. Friends or your local Wildlife Trust may be able to recommend a local contractor. As with

2 Choosing a site
In addition to the usual factors of shade, aspect and slope, extra care needs to be taken when selecting the site for a large pond. If you have a large, wet field, check that it contains no rare species or species-rich communities before destroying any of it to form a pond; it may be

Large winter pond

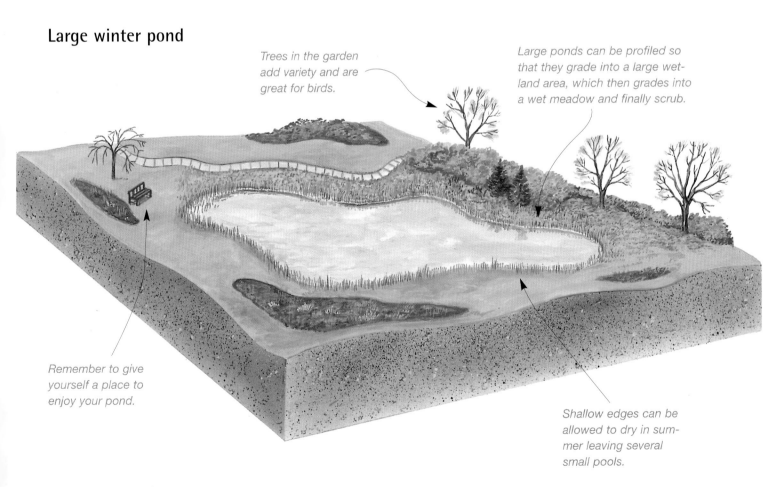

Trees in the garden add variety and are great for birds.

Large ponds can be profiled so that they grade into a large wetland area, which then grades into a wet meadow and finally scrub.

Remember to give yourself a place to enjoy your pond.

Shallow edges can be allowed to dry in summer leaving several small pools.

better to create your lake in the neighbouring field, thus maximizing the value to wildlife. An adequate water supply is vital, since filling a lake from a tap is not really feasible. A lake needs either an inflow of water or groundwater. Unless you know how to measure the water quantity available for your site, consult a hydrologist. A specialist pond contractor should be able to carry out a hydrological survey for you. Inflows, particularly in farming areas, often have excessive quantities of nutrients. A reedbed sited where water enters the pond can mop-up some of the incoming nutrients and help to prevent the pond turning into green-algal soup.

3 Marking out the position
Make scaled sketches of the pond's shape as guidance for marking out its position on the ground. The contractor will be able to identify the soil type, locate the best water source and, if necessary, mark out the shape of the pond based on your sketches.

4 Removing the topsoil
Topsoil will usually sit over the clay layer. Topsoil will not hold water, so should be removed to be spread over the margins of the pond or, if it is very rich in nutrients, used elsewhere in the garden.

5 Profile
The profile of a large lake is critical, but, even with a detailed sketch, will need to be explained carefully to the digger driver and to the contract manager (they may be the same person), and even then it is best to oversee the work. Digger drivers may take a pride in producing a symmetrical geometric shape, even if this is not what you want, as they are probably used to civil-engineering projects rather than conservation work. The contractor may need to dig a temporary ditch to divert water away from the site whilst the pond is being constructed. This will require permission from the appropriate environmental regulators.

6 Creating a watertight lining
The clay needs to be puddled, by running vehicles backwards and forwards over the base, to make it watertight (see *Puddled clay* on page 20).

7 Checking shape and level
Most diggers have built-in instruments for land-level measurement that tell the driver when a pre-determined depth has been reached. The levels around the edge of a large project

Above: *Excavators make light work of even the largest lined ponds.*

Above: *Use a lining for less ambitious large ponds. Fill it with a little water to stretch it into place.*

Above: *Plant a variety of plant species around the edges to help a pond become established.*

Below top: *Profile of the pond illustrated on pages 28 and below.*

Below bottom: *Having a variety of depths provides habitats for many different species.*

such as a lake will usually be checked using a theodolite (tripod with sights that, when used in tandem with a pole, allows the recording of precise heights). Make sure that the contractor knows that you want to see the profile and shape before the pond is finished.

8 Adding water
Start filling the pond with water by unblocking the inflow or by blocking the ditch

that you created to drain the site during construction. Leave the water to settle for at least three weeks; there may be an initial algal bloom, but this should clear naturally. Leaving the water also allows any silt to settle to the bottom of the new lake or pond.

9 Planting
You may wish to leave the large central areas to colonize naturally, but it is a good idea

Profile of a large pond

Deeper areas will remain wet all year round and provide refuge for fish and aquatic species.

Shallow central areas will dry out every summer and keep the ponds apart in all but the wettest winters. Shallow areas that dry out in summer are great for wetland plants and rare invertebrates.

Middle depth areas should dry out in some years and not in others. These areas are good for Great Crested Newts as they stay fish-free in all but the wettest years.

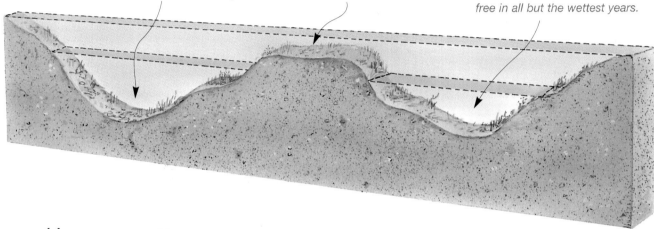

Large pond in summer

Several small pools form in the hollows as water evaporates in summer months.

A large wetland forms around each pool.

The deepest part forms a large pond in summer.

The central area remains exposed except in the wettest winters.

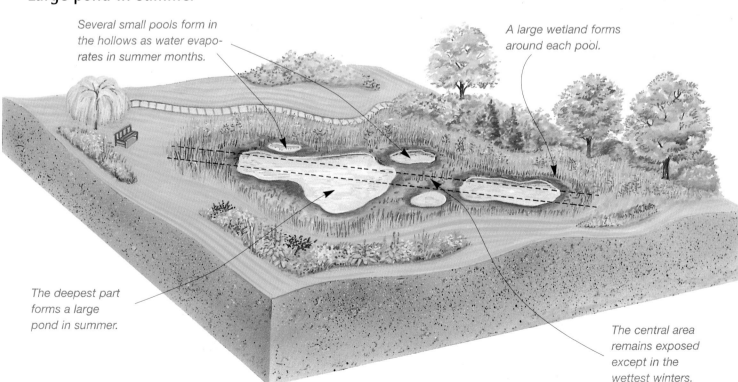

Left: *Having running water in your pond, such as a fountain, will keep it oxygenated. Surrounding your pond with a variety of plants will attract more wildlife into the garden.*

to plant some of the banks and shallows. For a large project, you should order plants from a specialist stockist, who should be contacted well in advance of the project, and set a delivery date.

You may need help with the planting, and this is best supplied by friends, family and local volunteers who have an interest in the lake and its potential. For ideas on what to plant and when see *Pond Plants* on pages 42 to 51.

10 Making wildlife-friendly borders
It would be a shame to have a barren desert of arable fields or concrete surrounding your lake or series of ponds. Once the pond is planted, the rest of the garden, park or field can be made more wildlife friendly, by judicious tree-planting or the creation of other habitats (see *Fantastic features* on page 32) to put the lake or ponds into a natural setting.

Fantastic features

If you want to maximize the wildlife in your garden, it is worth putting a little effort into the land around your pond. Many creatures spend only part of their lives in the water: frogs and toads visit the pond mainly to breed, while dragonflies and damselflies spend their adult lives out of the water. Grass Snakes will visit a pond to feed, but only if they have somewhere to live and overwinter. Birds will be attracted to drink and bathe at your pond only if they have suitable places nearby to feed, perch and nest.

Bird and bat boxes

Many of our garden birds are woodland species that are encouraged into gardens by the provision of bird-tables and feeders. In the gardens of old and country houses, there are usually mature trees and shrubs, ivy-covered walls and gaps under eaves for nesting and roosting sites. In the gardens of modern houses, young trees and well-pointed brickwork offer little or no opportunity for even the most enterprising species to make nests. Wildlife gardeners encourage trees to grow and plant ivy to cover walls, but the best ways of attracting visitors to your garden is to provide food, water and artificial nest sites.

Nest boxes come in all shapes and sizes, designed to attract species ranging from Blue Tits to Barn Owls. When choosing a box, pick one appropriate for the species likely to visit your garden. Ask for one made from sustainably harvested wood. It is best to use a specialist supplier, since those sold by some garden centres are too small and have holes through which even a small bird could not squeeze.

If you are fond of DIY, it is easy to build your own. The size and shape of the box, the precise size of the entrance hole, the height above ground level and position of the box all depend upon what you want to attract to your box. Robins, Spotted Flycatchers and wagtails need a box with a large entrance; tits and Pied Flycatchers need a smaller hole (different sizes for different species); owls and Kestrels need

Below: Making bird boxes and bat boxes is quite simple. All that is needed is some basic carpentry skills.

215mm

Making bird and bat boxes

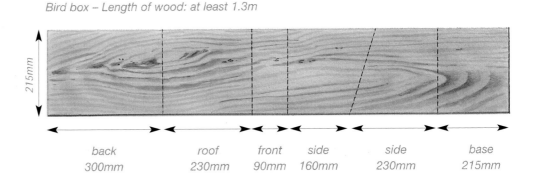

Bird box – Length of wood: at least 1.3m

215mm

back	roof	front	side	side	base
300mm	230mm	90mm	160mm	230mm	215mm

150mm

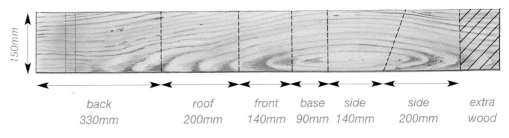

Bat box – Length of wood: at least 1.1m

150mm

back	roof	front	base	side	side	extra wood
330mm	200mm	140mm	90mm	140mm	200mm	

large boxes. If you need advice, consult your local Wildlife Trust or the Royal Society for the Protection of Birds (RSPB).

It is also worth considering the erection of bat boxes. Bats are a joy to watch, as they swoop down from on high to then skim over water to feed on insects. Your wildlife garden pond could provide them with an insect-rich haven.

Bat boxes should be placed 3–5m above the ground or even higher, on a tree, wall or post. The bats need a clear flightpath to the box entrance. If possible, site three boxes, one facing north one south-west and one south-east, for use at different times of year. You can check for signs of bats by looking for droppings and by carefully lifting the lid. If you find bats, you must telephone a statutory conservation agency (see page 77). Such organisations will give you advice and, by applying for a bat-worker's licence, you can legally check up on your bats.

Food and feeders
Providing food not only makes a difference to how many birds you see in your garden, but also affects how many survive the winter. Other animals, such as Hedgehogs, will also benefit from being provided with food. There are two considerations: what wildlife you want to feed and how best to feed it. Scattering food on the ground is simple, but is as likely to feed dogs, cats, rats and mice as it is to attract the wildlife that you want to encourage.

For birds, a range of different feeders and different foods will attract a range of species to your garden. Tits will come to feed on peanuts

Left: Ponds provide a rich source of insects, flowers and seeds, which are all good for Great Tits with a hungry family to feed.

or sunflower seeds in a wire basket, suspended from a tree, hooked onto the house or hung from a special post. These baskets have the advantage that the birds have to hang on the feeder to get at the nuts, so you get a good view of them, and they are out of reach of ground predators. Nuts are very attractive to squirrels so – unless you live in a region with native Red Squirrels and want to encourage them – erect slippery domes above hanging feeders to discourage the ingenious non-native Grey Squirrels.

HOW TO MAKE BIRD BOXES AND BAT BOXES

Small open-fronted **bird boxes** suitable for Dippers and Pied Wagtails can be made from a 1.5m length of 15mm by 215mm plank of untreated soft wood.

Cut the various sections from the continuous plank as shown in the diagram opposite. You will need six pieces: a back, a front, two sides, a base and a roof. Cut the sides on a 45° slope. Drill holes about 15mm from the top and bottom of the back. (These will be used to fix your bird box to a tree or wall.) Nail or screw all the pieces except the roof together. Form a hinge between the back and the roof using a piece of rubber or leather.

Bat boxes are similar to bird boxes, but instead of a front hole they have a gap

underneath for the bats to fly into.

Make a bat box from a 1.2m length of 25mm by 150mm plank of rough-sawn untreated soft wood. Again, cut the various sections from the continuous plank as shown in the diagram opposite. As with the bird box, you will need six pieces: a back, a front, two sides, a base and a roof. Cut the sides on a 45° slope. Drill holes about 15mm from the top and bottom of the back.

Nail or screw the front, base and sides together and then nail or screw this to the back. Leave a 50mm slit at the base of the box for the bats to enter. Form the roof hinge between the back and the roof in the same manner as with the bird box.

EQUIPMENT

- Plank of 1.5m soft wood
- Ruler
- Pencil
- Drill
- Saw
- Nails or screws
- Hammer or screwdriver
- Strong rubber or leather

Right: *Wildflower meadows are a larder for bees and other insects and provide a riot of colour. It is easy to create one in even the smallest garden. Ox-eye Daisies dominate this small meadow.*

Fill your feeders regularly, with a mixture of seeds, cereals and nuts. Sunflower seeds and peanuts are easy to obtain, cheap and full of energy for birds. It is, however, best to obtain food from a specialist supplier of certified wildlife food (see page 76).

Wildflowers and wonderful weeds

Leaving a strip of grass to seed or a border to remain unweeded and unplanted will allow wild flowers, grasses and herbs to come in. Sowing native wildflower seeds on a bare patch of soil can give a spectacular meadow effect even

within just a few square metres. Wildflowers that some people would call weeds will encourage a whole host of butterflies, moths and attractive insects to your garden. A range of bulbs and plants can be added to the edges of a pond to create attractive damp spots for your emerging pond life. Snowdrops will enhance damp, shady edges if the soil is rich and moist.

Compost and dead wood

Tidy gardeners who rake up and burn every bit of dead wood and leaves are the enemy of wildlife. Leaves provide a good mulch, to stop your plants

Below: *See how to plan your garden from an upstairs window. Work with what is already there, especially mature native trees, as they will take decades to replace.*

Planning the features around your pond

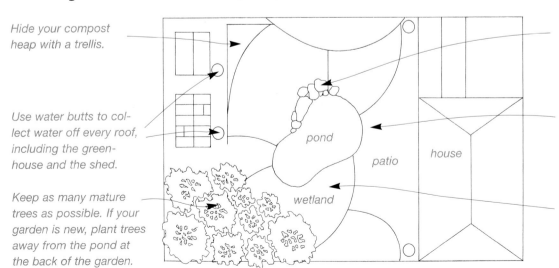

Hide your compost heap with a trellis.

Use water butts to collect water off every roof, including the greenhouse and the shed.

Keep as many mature trees as possible. If your garden is new, plant trees away from the pond at the back of the garden.

Site your rockery to catch the south-facing sun, giving maximum opportunities for basking reptiles.

Face one side of the pond onto a patio, creating great opportunities for watching wildlife.

Site the wetland in the overspill area of the pond. Shade the back of the wetland with trees, creating a great place for ferns.

pond

patio

house

wetland

drying out, or, if left to rot further, a beautifully rich compost, so do not burn or bin them. Piles of leaves and grass clippings can be made to look tidy by putting them in a fenced area with a net wire or wooden lid to hold them in place. These dead leaf and garden waste heaps not only provide you with free compost, but also provide homes for overwintering toads and Slow-worms, and, if you are really lucky, a Grass Snake will lay its eggs in the warm centre of the rotting leaves.

Leaving log piles creates refuges from hot days and winter weather for toads, as well as providing food for a whole host of invertebrates that feed on dead wood. Many mosses, lichens and fungi also live on dead wood. Piles of leaves or branches will provide homes for Hedgehogs. As well as being one of the most delightful snuffly creatures to find in your garden, these nocturnal wanderers will eat your slugs.

Rockeries

Rockeries have gone a little out of fashion in the fickle world of garden design, but it is difficult to beat a good, well-established rockery for wildlife interest. They are visually attractive, provide perches for birds and homes for a range of creatures from voles to invertebrates such as woodlice. Never dig up or take rocks from the countryside: you may be breaking the law and will certainly be damaging wildlife habitat. Bare-rock areas, such as limestone pavement, are rare and precious in the UK. If you do create a rockery from commercially available material, ensure that this is from a reputable source.

A pile of rocks will look more natural than an even scatter, and will form more nooks and crannies for wildlife. Having the bottom stones jutting out into the water will look great, and will also provide perches for birds that come to drink. Do not place large stones or rocks straight onto the lining, but ensure they are padded by soil or some protective matting. If you plan to have large heavy stones around the pond, add a little extra liner at this point. Some gaps between the larger rocks can be filled with soil and planted with native plants such as heathers, which will attract bees and butterflies to their delicate purple flowers.

Below: What you establish around your pond is almost as important as what you put in it. A few extra features will increase the variety of wildlife visiting your pond.

Fantastic features

Compost heaps are nurseries for Grass Snakes.

nest box

Short grass can be good for birds and beetles.

Rockeries are hotels for reptiles and amphibians.

wildflower meadow

A bench is a good place to rest and enjoy the wildlife.

Bare mud is good for birds to come and drink.

dead wood

Pond Maintenance

The range of wildlife that lives and visits a pond depends upon the way that the pond is managed. Each pond in a wetland complex needs to be maintained slightly differently, to reflect the different communities of plants and animals that have colonized them. Managing ponds involves making choices and decisions.

Many myths surround the definition of 'good pond management'. Some guides recommend clearing vegetation from ponds every year: raking, pulling, dividing and cutting vegetation to maintain lots of open water. All this disturbance is not good for the wildlife and is aimed mainly at pond owners who wish to keep ornamental fish.

One of the most important parts of pond management is observation. Watch what is happening in your pond and keep a wildlife diary of wildlife that you see. Note down what produces flowers and when. Also note how the water levels rise and drop throughout the seasons. This record of how your pond is changing will help you to decide whether you need to carry out any management and what kind you should do and, more importantly, when.

Managing plants

Water and wetland plants can extend quickly out from the shallow edges until they cover the whole pond. This is no bad thing. The luxuriant growth of a variety of wetland plants is one of the joys of a wildlife pond. Some open water at the deepest part of the pond is good for fish, newts and free-swimming invertebrates.

Tall emergent plants can extend from the edge far out into the pond, reducing the space and light for submerged and floating-leaved plants. Where one or two species are starting to dominate the pond, it may be time for a little plant management. In most cases, pulling and lifting of vegetation is the best option and, as with all management, 'little and often' is almost always better than drastic plant clearance. Small-scale lifting may also remove small amounts of silt, which will reduce the rate the pond silts up, reducing or even preventing the need for de-silting.

In winter, thin out submerged aquatic plants by raking them. Winter is also a good time to trim back any dead or dying plants before they fall into the pond and rot. Always remove plants carefully, as some very uncommon wetland plants, such as Pillwort (*Pilularia globulifera*) and Starfruit (*Damasonium alisma*), can easily be overlooked, as they are small and low growing.

Ponds can become completely covered in duckweed, blocking out light and preventing other plants from growing. Use a long-handled net in late spring to skim duckweed off the surface, but take care to check for

invertebrates. Indeed, all vegetation removed from a pond should always be placed in a tray or mesh above the pond or at the pond edge to drain for a few hours or overnight, to allow wildlife caught up in the pond weed to escape back into the pond. The weed should not be left to drain for longer than a few hours, as it will rot and release toxins and nutrients back into the pond.

De-silting

Regular maintenance – raking fallen leaves, and periodically thinning vegetation – and good design should ensure that silting is very slow, so that de-silting is seldom necessary. When it is, drain the water from a small pond and carefully scoop out the silt into a bucket. Lift and store a few specimens of each plant temporarily in buckets or plastic bags. The best time of year for this operation is from autumn until December, when most pond species will be inactive. Many animals will, however, be overwintering in the mud, so rescue anything that wriggles in the black ooze. If possible, also retain the top layer of the silt on a board, keep it wet and replace it once the de-silting is over. The remaining silt will make an excellent fertilizer elsewhere in the garden.

With a larger pond, one option is to partially drain it using a bucket or a siphon tube, leaving some water as a refuge. Silt and excessive plant growth can then be cleared from, say, one-quarter of the pond, and this operation repeated every other year. Stream-fed lakes should have silt traps that can be cleared regularly, usually every year, either by hand or by using small diggers.

Algae

When ponds turn blue-green, green or red, or get covered in green slime, it is all down to tiny microscopic algae. There are three main types of algae that cause problems: blue-green algae (Cyanobacteria), single-celled green algae, and filamentous green algae. Blue-green algae often occur in new ponds or in spring,

forming a foam or scum on the pond, causing the water to smell unpleasant and producing toxins that can be poisonous to animals living in or drinking the water. Blooms of single-celled algae give pond water a pea-soup appearance.

Above: As well as being a beautiful flower, lilies provide homes for invertebrates and perches for birds, such as this Grey Wagtail. But beware – plant them in baskets to prevent total takeover.

Left: When de-silting your pond, keep an eye out for invertebrates, such as these Water Scorpions, lurking at the bottom in the mud.

Above: *Green, gooey and ghastly – algal blooms are an all-too-frequent sight in ponds. Fight back using the barley straw technique.*

Filamentous green algae create a slimy layer of floating strands that look like cotton, commonly called blanket weed. All forms of algal bloom can block out the light to other, higher plants in the pond, killing them. When they rot, the oxygen content of the water is depressed, which can kill fish and the more sensitive invertebrates, such as mayfly nymphs and freshwater mussels.

The best way to control algal growth is to reduce nutrient levels, by limiting the addition of nutrients on surrounding land, or by preventing nutrient-rich water from entering the pond.

Removal of blanket weed – by raking it from large ponds or winding it around a stick in small ponds – will also get rid of some nutrients. A wildlife-friendly way of treating all types of algal bloom is to submerge a netted bundle of barley straw in the pond. Well-dried barley straw produces chemicals that limit algal growth, but do not affect most of the other plants and animals in the pond. The straw takes one or two weeks to become active in hot weather (>20°C), and even longer in cold weather, so will not clear algae overnight, but it remains effective until it is completely rotted.

Leaves

Skim leaves from the surface of the water with an ordinary garden rake or a long-handled net. Unless this is done regularly, the leaves will sink to the bottom of the pond and removing them will stir up silt, making the water murky. On a large lake, a rowing boat and a boom can be used. As already noted, leave such vegetation at the edge for a few hours, so that small creatures clinging to them can crawl or fall back into the water. Add the skimmed leaves to your compost heap.

Repairing leaks

Repairing leaks is quite difficult, so prevention is better than cure. A well-planned and well-maintained pond should last for many years without leaking. Accidents do happen, however, and linings do wear out.

First, double-check that there is a leak, and that it is not just a natural drop in water level due to evaporation and plant transpiration. Fill the pond up in the early evening: if the water level drops overnight, you have a leak.

USING BARLEY STRAW TO CONTROL ALGAE

The amount of barley straw you use is very important; if you apply too little it will have no effect on your algal problem, if you apply too much you may deoxygenate the pond and kill all your wildlife! The amount is related to the surface area of your pond. To work out the surface area of a rectangular or square pond multiply the length by the width, for a circular pond muliply pie squared by the radius of the pond.

Initally you need approximately 50g of straw per square metre of surface water. The second application is applied once the first straw is rotted, this should be 25g per square metre and the third application should be 10g per square metre. So for a 5m long and 3m wide pond you would need 15 x 50g = 750g of straw for the initial application, then 15 x 25g = 375g of straw for the second application. All further applications to this pond would be 15 x 10 = 150g of straw.

If the water is turbid or muddy it will be necessary to add about twice as much straw. The best way to apply straw depends on the size of the pond. In small ponds with no flowing water where only a few grams are needed the straw can be stuffed into a net bag or an old stocking or simply tied neatly with string. Do not pack the straw in tightly but let it float loosely inside the net. Bales of straw only really work if the water is flowing – they are too large and too tightly packed for garden ponds. To ensure the bag stays on the surface insert a piece of polystyrene or cork to help it float. To ensure this light package does not blow away use a stone as a weight. Once the straw has rotted it can be removed and replaced.

Left: *Leaves floating on the water can be a real pain for the garden owner. Raking them out will save your pond and give you lots of compost as a bonus.*

Secondly, find the leak. Allow the water level to drop and then examine the liner about 10cm above and 5cm below this level all around the pond. If no puncture is visible, fill the pond to above the level of the leak, fill a squeeze bottle with water and a bright red food dye, and squirt this in small bursts every few centimetres around the pond. The dye should move towards the site of the leak. Once this is located, drain the pond to a few centimetres below the leak and allow the leaking area to dry completely before attempting any repair. Remember to look around the whole pond, as there may be more than one leak, and mark every leak that you find with brightly coloured tape or other marker.

Always drain water slowly to allow animals to seek refuge in deeper water. If you have to drain the whole pond, many of the plants and animals will survive temporarily in buckets and pots.

Repair butyl-lined ponds by pushing powdered bentonite (see page 20) into the gaps; when water is added, the bentonite expands and seals the leak (though this is not as easy as it sounds, and powdered bentonite can clog the gills of fish). Alternatively, aquatic sealants can be satisfactory, but aquatic glues, such as Aquasure, are even better. Dry the damaged area thoroughly and roughen it with fine sandpaper before applying any sealant. For a small hole, simply squeeze the glue all around the puncture;

for a larger hole or tear, try gluing a patch over the aperture. Allow the glue to set and dry properly before refilling the pond. Wear gloves when applying glues and sealants and, since some may give off noxious fumes, wear a face mask if sealing a large area. Pond-repair kits containing sandpaper, repair patches, resin, gloves and applicator, and costing £15–20, are available from water-garden specialists. These are sometimes said to be suitable for fibreglass, concrete and all flexible liners, but are probably effective only with flexible liners or very small leaks.

Flexible liners may perish with age, and may develop a new leak as soon as an old one is plugged. Relining is then necessary. Remove the old liner, check that the protective under-layer is still in good condition (or replace the matting or newspapers and top up the sand) and then fit a new liner. Leave the water for a few days to settle before putting the plants and animals back into the pond.

Clay is easy to repair by adding more clay and re-puddling. Unless the pH is low or there are large concentrations of mineral salts, bentonite may also be used to repair a leaking clay pond, applying it to large areas if the exact site of the leak cannot be found. If the leak is caused through temporary drying and cracking, the clay may swell and reseal the crack by itself. To prevent re-cracking, keep the water level high.

SAFETY FIRST

Put safety first: do not reach out too far, and when carrying out maintenance in deep water always have someone with you.

All gardeners should have at least one water butt, to save water from the roof of the house, and also any outbuilding or greenhouse. Use the water to top up a pond in summer. Cold water from a butt could be a shock to animals in a warm pond, so allow the water to warm up in the sun before adding it to the pond. If the relative levels and distance allow, it may be possible to transfer the water from a butt directly into the pond via a hidden hosepipe, thereby taking immediate advantage of every rain shower.

Uninvited guests

Not everything that comes to garden ponds is welcome. As with other wetlands, ponds are susceptible to invasive non-native species: plants and animals that have been introduced from a different area, habitat, country or even continent. While the vast majority of garden species remain happily in gardens doing no damage to the countryside, a few do cause severe problems for our native species.

Garden ponds are a major source of invasive species spreading, since well-meaning but misguided pond-owners transfer them to the wild. They can also cause severe problems within the pond, since it can be difficult and expensive to eradicate them.

Of the many non-native plants that can cause havoc in a wildlife pond, four of the most common are:

Polythene and PVC liners are very hard to repair, although masking tape may help.

A brick or concrete pond is also very difficult to repair: the cracked area has to be chipped away and re-concreted or filled with a chemical sealant. This usually requires professional attention, since inexpert work may result in even worse cracks.

A drying pond

It is a hot summer and your pond is drying out. What should you do? If you have several ponds, let some of them dry out partially or completely (unless they contain fish). The area uncovered as a pond dries is valuable for wildlife, and provides habitats for rare plants and places for birds to feed on insects.

- **Floating Pennywort** (*Hydrocotyle ranunculoides*) is a native plant of North America. It was introduced to Britain as an ornamental pond plant in the 1980s. It can grow up to 8m in a single summer, at the amazing rate of up to 20cm per day.
  - **Australian Swamp Stonecrop** or **New Zealand Pigmyweed** (*Crassula helmsii*) was introduced as an oxygenating plant for aquaria.
  - **Parrot's Feather** (*Myriophyllum aquaticum*), related to our native water-milfoils, comes from South America, but was introduced as an ornamental plant in the 1960s.
  - **Water Fern** (*Azolla filiculoides*) arrived from North and South America as a weed with other exotic ornamental species.

All four will out-compete native species and can be disastrous for your pond wildlife. Parrot's Feather is attractive, but when it is the only plant in your pond you can get a little sick of it. Numbers of native insects will also be reduced when the plants that they feed on and live under are eliminated.

Floating Pennywort, Australian Swamp Stonecrop and Water Fern all form thick mats that can smother native plants, which rot and die, using up oxygen in the water; in time, this can kill all the fish and most of the invertebrates in a pond. The dense, floating mats can look like solid ground, and can even be a hazard to unwary children or pets.

The maxim that prevention is better than cure is particularly true for the control of invasive species. For a new pond, buy only native species of pond plants and allow animals to colonize naturally. If, however, you are unlucky enough to have acquired one or more of these invasive species in your pond, what should you do? The often over-looked first step is to make quite certain that you have correctly identified the species. Leaflets on the identification of invasive plant species are available from the Centre for Aquatic Plant Management (CAPM), fact sheets describing both native and non-native amphibians and reptiles from the organization Froglife, and fact sheets on species most likely to be found in garden ponds from The Wildlife Trusts' UK Office.

Control options

To get rid of unwanted plant species, there are four theoretical options:
• Physical control
• Environmental control
• Biological control
• Chemical control
Cutting, pulling or raking are the most common physical-control methods used in garden ponds. Pulling works well for rooted plants, since, although it is back-breaking work, it removes the entire plant. Plants that grow from tiny fragments, such as Floating Pennywort, Australian Swamp Stonecrop and Water Fern, will, however, merely be spread by physical methods intended to have the opposite effect and so one of the other methods would be more appropriate.

Environmental controls include shading problem plants with taller plants, smothering them with polythene, or increasing water flow. None of these options are very effective, since shading or smothering will kill other plants and animals, probably before the problem plants are affected,

and increasing water flow may simply transfer the problem downstream.

Animals that eat plants can sometimes be used to provide biological control. There are often no native animals that eat the non-native plants to control them effectively, which is why they become problems. Grass Carp (*Ctenopharyngodon idella*), an introduced fish, will eat most aquatic plants, but is unlikely to survive the low oxygen levels generated by problem plants and will itself become a problem.

If possible avoid using pesticides, but this may be the only option for some species. Only a few chemicals are approved for use in or near water, the least harmful of these being preparations of glyphosate (but even this mild, biodegradable chemical can cause problems for amphibians, so it should not be sprayed in spring). Always follow the manufacturer's instructions and, if you are unsure, seek advice or employ a qualified specialist to spray the problem plants.

Above: *Grey Herons may visit your pond in autumn and winter. Fish owners net their ponds, but wildlife gardeners have nothing to fear from herons as wildlife ponds have few fish, most of which are well concealed in vegetation.*

Pond Plants

Planting appropriate plants in a new pond will not only make it look attractive, but will also provide homes for many invertebrates. When flowers appear, they will attract nectar-seeking insects and, in consequence, also other wildlife.

Above: *Plant Water Mint at the edge of your pond.*

Planting zones

An unlined wildlife pond near another wetland does not need to be planted, except, perhaps, to protect its banks from erosion. You can sit back and watch nature go to work, enjoying the changes as different waves of plants and animals colonize one after another. A lined pond, excavated in the family garden, does, however, need to be planted.

Most people introduce a pond in order to add appeal to their garden. Although it is fun to observe the slow evolution from a mud pit through early algae and stoneworts to the arrival of marginals, such patience is not everyone's cup of tea. Planting a pond will also reduce (although not eliminate) the risk of it being taken over by unwelcome non-native invasive plants.

Establishing appropriate plants is one of the most enjoyable parts of creating a wildlife pond and allows you to be somewhat creative. Try to mimic the natural ponds that you have used for your inspiration, but be realistic – you may not have the right soil conditions or the right size pond for some plants.

Where to plant in your pond

Deep-water zone

Submerged plants are the oxygenators and need to be planted first, e.g. Rigid Hornwort, Spiked Water-milfoil, Common Water-starwort, Willowmoss.

Floating-leaved plants are perennial favourites, e.g. Broad-leaved Pondweed, White Water-lily, Yellow Water-lily, Water-soldier.

Shallow-water zone

Mix up tall and low-growing plants, e.g. Arrowhead, Brooklime, Mare's Tail, Water Forget-me-not.

Wetland and pond-edge zone

The most species-rich parts of the pond, e.g. Yellow Iris, Water Plantain.

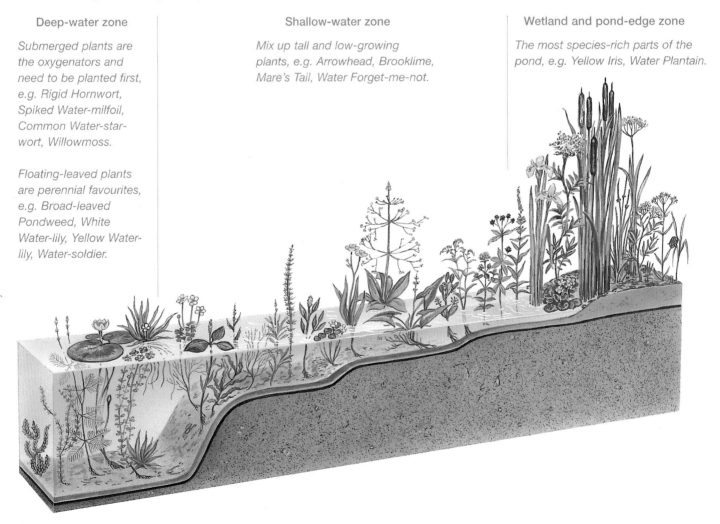

Left: *Tall emergent plants have a tendency to take over ponds. Make sure you create more open edges by mixing in clumps of smaller plants.*

In this account, I have sorted pond plants into the zones that they occupy in natural ponds: (a) deep water, (b) shallow water, and (c) wetland and pond edge. The deep-water plants are further subdivided into those that are submerged and those that float or have floating leaves. In reality, there is no obvious line between zones, which merge into one another and are often mixed up together. For instance, Yellow Iris can grow in standing water or in the marshy margins, and Water Mint will spread all over the place.

Just have fun with your planting and remember to buy native plants: they are the easiest to grow, they look great, and they are what native insects and other native wildlife need to feed on.

Propagating pond plants

If the native plants that you want are not available from your nearest nursery, garden centre or other stockist, you can try to propagate them from the stock in a friend's pond. Spring is the best time to divide marginal pond, wetland and most aquatic plants, as this is when they are starting to grow, and they then have all summer to become fully established in your pond before the winter sets in.

Many clump-forming plants, such as Marsh Marigold, can simply be broken up by hand or with a fork – use the young, healthy-looking parts to establish new clumps. Discard the interior parts of the old clumps, as they may be exhausted. Replant the new pieces into an established pond immediately or grow them in pots first, if you wish to check for disease, other hitch-hiking plants or parasites.

Dividing creeping plants, such as Flowering-rush, Bogbean, Water Mint and Lesser Celandine, is simple. The roots of these plants have a scrambling habit and can be increased by dividing the horizontal roots into sections, ensuring that each separate part has a healthy bud or young shoot and roots. On Flowering-rush, there is a small bulb-like formation, called a bulbil, at the base of the hard, woody roots where it meets the leaves. Ensure each divided section contains a bulbil, and plant them in wet compost and cover until healthy roots develop. The new plants can then be replanted.

Water-lilies, Marsh Marigold and many other marsh plants can be grown from seed, but others are best propagated vegetatively, using stems, rhizomes or division. Fritillary grows from bulbs, so you can simply split them and replant them in autumn, as you would with daffodils or other bulbs.

Below: *Marsh Marigolds are a must for any wildlife pond. They provide a great splash of yellow in spring, attracting early insects to your pond.*

Deep-water zone – submerged plants

To reach this zone, you have to cross the shallower zones, so plant this area first, to avoid trampling newly-established plants.

Many submerged plants are oxygenators and are essential for many other plants and animals; they will be amongst the first plants to colonize

any new pond. Many books recommend introducing Canadian Pondweed (*Elodea canadensis*) to a new pond. It is indeed an excellent oxygenator, and it grows exuberantly, and can be seen all over Britain's countryside ponds. It is actually far better to opt for a native plant. Suitable for waters that are alkaline, Spiked Water-milfoil or Whorled Water-milfoil are delicate, beautiful plants that will grow and oxygenate just as well as the non-native Canadian Pondweed. They appear to die off in winter, but in reality overwinter in the bottom of the pond.

Water-starworts are smaller than water-milfoils, but have very attractive bright-green, delicate whorls of leaves. There are many species of water-starwort, appropriate for habitats ranging from running water to still water. A mix of species will provide the best balance, as well as a more interesting appearance.

Left: *A Freshwater Louse is one of the many invertebrates that will be found lurking in among submerged plants.*

Below: *Water-milfoil is a beautiful flower and will breathe life into your pond – a much more interesting oxygenator than Canadian Pondweed.*

In the wild, water-milfoils, water-starworts and pondweeds are amongst the most common aquatic plants. It is, however, surprisingly difficult to find these plants in garden or even aquarium centres. All of them will grow from a small portion, so propagating them from a friend's pond is the best way. If all your friends have only Canadian Pondweed in their ponds, then you may have to contact a specialist supplier. You need to buy only a very small amount, as these plants grow very well under the right conditions. If they begin to choke your pond, they will tolerate sensitive, judicious cutting or pulling, by hand or with a rake. Clear only a small amount at a time and, of course, allow all the invertebrates attached to them to escape back into the pond.

The planting guide below gives some examples of submerged plants, with tips on how, when and why to plant them.

PLANTING GUIDE – SUBMERGED PLANTS

Species	How deep to plant them	Where to plant them	Notes
Alternate Water-milfoil (*Myriophyllum alternifolium*)	In water up to 2m deep	Sun to partial shade	Much pickier than Spiked Water-milfoil: likes slightly acid, clear water.
Common Water-starwort (*Callitriche stagnalis*)	In water up to 1m deep	Sun to partial shade	Likes a flow of water, but can grow in still water.
Curled Pondweed (*Potamogeton crispus*)	In water 75cm deep, sometimes deeper	Sun to partial shade	Not fussy about soil or water nutrients, but needs clear water.
Fennel Pondweed (*Potamogeton pectinatus*)	In water from 50cm to 2.5m deep	Sun to partial or even full shade	Quite adaptable and can tolerate more turbidity than other submerged plants.
Rigid Hornwort (*Ceratophyllum demersum*)	In depths up to 1m, sometimes deeper	Sun to partial shade	Quite adaptable and a really good oxygenator.
Short-leaved Water-starwort (*Callitriche truncata*)	In water up to 1m deep	Sun to partial shade	Likes still water, but is rare in the wild.
Soft Hornwort (*Ceratophyllum submersum*)	In shallow waters	Sun or shade	Much less adaptable than Rigid Hornwort, but is a really good oxygenator.
Spiked Water-milfoil (*Myriophyllum spicatum*)	In water up to 2m deep	Sun to partial shade	Very adaptable and can grow in both still and flowing waters, but likes clear, alkaline waters best.
Whorled Water-milfoil (*Myriophyllum verticillatum*)	In shallow water or up to 1.5m deep	Sun to partial shade	Likes still water and fine peaty soils, though will grow in mineral soils.
Willowmoss (*Fontinalis antipyretica*)	In water up to 2m deep	Sun to partial shade	This very unusual moss can grow in fast-flowing streams, but will survive in a clear pond. It can grow several metres long and is a great oxygenator.

PLANTING SUBMERGED PLANTS

Many species of submerged plants are so vigorous that you can just throw a small piece into the pond and it will grow. Plant the more sensitive species, such as the water-starworts, in a basket weighted down with stones. Lower the basket into the pond.

Deep-water zone – floating-leaved and free-floating plants

Plants rooted in the mud, but with their leaves floating, such as water-lilies, are very popular in garden ponds. Yellow Water-lily and White Water-lily are both native British plants, and Fringed Water-lily may be too. Garden and aquarium centres often sell non-native, cultivated varieties with flowers all sorts of gaudy pinks, which look out of place in a wildlife pond. The native species are both vigorous and hardy; in fact, they are more likely to take over the pond than to require the cosseting needed by some of the non-native varieties.

If your pond is large and you know someone with water-lilies, you can collect the seedpods and sow the seeds in your pond. Alternatively, cut a section of the rhizome root mat with buds during spring. This is very muddy work, you may need to do it with a saw, and you will make a temporary mess of your friend's pond. Budding rhizome, tied to a stone within a restricting basket at the bottom of your pond, can, however, develop into flowering lilies in the same summer. Unrestricted, any water-lily can take over a pond.

The floating leaves of water-lilies provide great hiding places for small fish, tadpoles and invertebrates, and grazing for pond snails. I have never yet seen a frog sitting on a lily pad, but I am assured that they do do so on occasions (grab your camera!). Of other floating-leaved plants, Broad-leaved Pondweed, with its attractive pinkish-green leaves, can commonly be seen covering lowland ponds.

Free-floating plants also provide animals with protection from sun and predators. Frogbit and Water-soldier are great, but some of the smaller free-floating plants, such as the duckweeds, can become a real problem. Most of the small free-floating plants sold by garden centres are non-

Below: With its spectacular giant white flowers, the White Water-lily is native to the UK and provides homes for snails, and shelter for tadpoles and small fish.

Above: Many species of water-crowfoots live only in running water, but Common Water-crowfoot is not fussy. It produces underwater leaves and buttercup-shaped leaves that float on the surface. In late spring it produces delicate white flowers covering the pond surface.

native, and they also often hitch a ride on native aquatic plants from the same sources. Check all plants carefully after purchase, and wash them to remove the hitch-hikers before putting them into your pond. It is far easier to avoid introducing an unwanted plant accidentally than it is to eliminate it once it has taken over your pond.

The planting guide below gives some examples of floating-leaved and free-floating plants, with tips on how, when and why to plant them. A good aquarist will probably stock some of the more common species, such as Broad-leaved Pondweed, the various water-lilies and the water-crowfoots.

PLANTING GUIDE – FLOATING-LEAVED AND FREE-FLOATING PLANTS

Species	Flower type and colour	When they flower	Where to plant them	Notes
Broad-leaved Pondweed (*Potamogeton natans*)	Small green	May–Aug	Full sun, in water from 30cm to 3m deep	Needs to be able to reach the surface to produce its flower spike. Has both under-water and above-water leaves. Prefers still, clear water.
Common Water-crowfoot (*Ranunculus aquatilis*)	Small, white, in profusion	Mar–May	Full sun, in water up to 50cm deep or more	Likes still or slow-flowing water, not too fussy about the soil, but is usually found in alkaline rather than acid waters.
Fringed Water-lily (*Nymphoides peltata*)	Yellow	June–Sept	Full sun, in water 50cm to 3m deep	Very pretty, but, like all water-lilies, capable of taking over a pond. Likes still water, with fine, peat or mineral soil.
Frogbit (*Hydrocharis morsus-ranae*)	White	July–Aug	Full sun, on top of or under water	Grows from runners overwintering as buds in mud at the bottom of the pond. Likes still, unpolluted water with high alkalinity.
Water-soldier (*Stratiotes aloides*)	White	July–Aug	Full sun, in shallow water or floating on deeper water	Unusual shape and very adaptable: can grow as free-floating, submerged or rooted, emergent plant.
Water-violet (*Hottonia palustris*)	Delicate mauve	May–June	Sun	When not in flower, can look like a water-milfoil.
White Water-lily (*Nymphaea alba*)	Large, spectacular, white	July–Aug	Full sun, in water up to 3m deep	Use to make an impact, but beware: it can take over a pond, so best planted in baskets. Likes still water.
Yellow Water-lily (*Nuphar lutea*)	Large, yellow	June–Aug	Full sun, in water up to 1.5 m deep	Not quite so spectacular as White Water-lily, but still amazing and equally capable of a pond take-over, so plant in a basket.

Above: *Snails have a terrible reputation for damaging aquatic plants, but many species are simply grazing on the algae that grow on the surface of plant leaves. This is a Wandering Snail (Lymnaea peregra).*

Shallow-water zone

The plants in shallow water are very important, since this is where most aquatic invertebrates hide or hunt their prey. It is a difficult area in which to plant successfully, since it is necessary to achieve a balance between the large, architectural plants, such as Flowering-rush and Water Plantain, and the smaller, low-growing species with pretty flowers, such as Water Forget-me-not.

Arrowhead is one of my favourite shallow-water plants: the flowers are not much to write home about, being small and delicate, but the leaves are large arrow shapes pointing up to the sky, and provide interest throughout the spring and summer.

If you like big, bright flowers, Yellow Iris or the loosestrifes are perfect. Yellow Iris has large yellow flowers and grows vigorously both in the water and into the marsh zone. Indeed, it sometimes grows a little too vigorously, especially for very small ponds, and you may need to dig it up and divide it (which is easy, and you can then supply all your friends).

Some emergent plants, such as Flowering-rush, bur-reeds, bulrushes and Bogbean will grow in deeper water. Bulrushes are particularly good in large ponds, as they provide nest sites, nesting material, food and shelter for waterfowl and for warblers. Rapidly spreading species, such as Common Reed, Branched Bur-reed and, especially, the bulrushes, can take

Right: Arrowhead's unusual flowers and leaves will add interest to your pond and attract many insects.

Below: Bogbean is one of the most structurally-pleasing wetland plants. It flowers in May to July and has amazing flowers that appear to be fraying at the edges.

Right: Flowering plants such as Greater Spearwort provide nectar for bees and other insects and seeds for birds.

over ponds. Greater Bulrush has the added disadvantage of fixing nitrogen, which can enrich the pond and may lead to excessive amounts of duckweed or algal blooms. Bur-reeds and bulrushes are too large (>1m tall) and too invasive for a small pond. If bulrushes do take over a pond, cut them back well below the water surface, using shears.

The planting guide below covers some of the most interesting native species with tips on how, when and why to plant them. The more common species, such as Yellow Iris and Water Mint, will probably be available in your local garden centre, and the others are usually stocked by specialist aquatic-plant suppliers; some addresses are given on page 76.

PLANTING GUIDE – SHALLOW-WATER PLANTS

Species	Plant height (cm)	Flower type and colour	When they flower	Where to plant them	Notes
Amphibious Bistort (*Polygonum amphibium*)	30-70 (long)	Large, pink	July-Sept	Full sun, on bank or floating on shallow or deep water	Really a shallow-water plant.
Arrowhead (*Sagittaria sagittifolia*)	30-80	Small, white	July-Aug	Sun, in shallow water, but will grow in deeper water	Great architectural plant, with pretty flowers and spectacular leaves.
Bogbean (*Menyanthes trifoliata*)	10-30	Fluffy, white	May-July	Full sun, in deep or shallow water	Can take over a pond, but is easy to trim and manage.
Branched Bur-reed (*Sparganium erectum*)	150	Green	June-Aug	Sun, in deeper water	Very vigorous, so do not plant in a small pond.
Brooklime (*Veronica beccabunga*)	20-30	Small, blue	May-Sept	Partial shade, in shallow water (<30cm deep)	Great for providing cover at the water's edge.
Floating Sweet-grass (*Glyceria fluitans*)	25-90	Silvery	May-Aug	Sun	Water Vole's favourite food.
Flowering-rush (*Butomus umbellatus*)	150	Pink	July-Sept	Sun, in shallow or deep water	From butterflies and dragonflies to birds – all love this beautiful plant.
Greater Spearwort (*Ranunculus lingua*)	60-90	Yellow	July-Sept	Sun, in shallow or deep water	Very vigorous and can take over shallow ponds of any size.
Lesser Bulrush (*Typha angustifolia*)	180-210	Huge brown spikes	June-July	Sun, in water up to 60cm deep	Very vigorous, so do not plant in a small pond.
Lesser Spearwort (*Ranunculus flammula*)	150	Yellow	May-Sept	Sun, in shallow water (<30cm deep)	Can take over a pond, so use with caution.
Water Forget-me-not (*Myosotis scorpioides*)	15-30	Delicate, blue	May-Sept	Partial shade, in shallow water (<30cm deep)	Provides rafts onto which insects often climb.
Water Mint (*Mentha aquatica*)	15-60	Pink	July-Oct	Sun or partial shade, in shallow water (<30cm deep)	Smells great, but plant it in a basket, as otherwise it will extend everywhere.
Water Plantain (*Alisma plantago-aquatica*)	30-90	Delicate white spikes	June-Aug	Sun or partial shade, in medium-depth water (<50cm)	A real beauty that can be planted straight into the soil and left alone.
Yellow Iris (*Iris pseudacorus*)	45-150	Huge, yellow	May-Aug	Sun or partial shade, in shallow water or on the bank	A 'must' for any water garden.

Wetland and pond-edge zone

The edge of the pond, as it grades from shallow water to wetland, is richer in plant species than any other area of the pond. It is also a very important area for invertebrates; many species of beetle like the wet margins. The abundance of flowers in marshes can provide food for butterflies and ensure colour in your garden from early spring until late autumn.

One of the best-known early flowering wetland plants is Marsh Marigold (also known as Kingcup or, my favourite, Mollyblobs). It is easy to grow, and brings a splash of bright yellow in early spring. Purple Loosestrife, which has huge spiked heads of bright pinkish-purple flowers throughout the summer and autumn, can grow to a height of over 1m. Another flowering giant is the Great Willowherb, which can grow to a height of 1.2m. Loosestrifes and willowherbs are very attractive to butterflies, bees and other nectar-loving insects (and are so much more interesting than Buddleia).

The planting guide opposite covers only a small sample of the many pond-edge plants. They are more readily available from garden centres than are truly aquatic plants. Wildflower seed mixes are available on-line, by mail order and even at some local shops. Wildflower-specialist merchants sell wet-meadow mixes perfect for the pond-edge or wetland zone. You can also collect seeds from friends' gardens.

Many of these plants grow from runners, while others, like the fritillaries, grow from bulbs. These can easily be propagated, and you can supply the rest of your garden from just a few initial plants.

If you are making a large wetland area, incorporate a few scattered stepping-stones, to allow access to the pond-edge and to the wetland plants without trampling. If this area is lined, make sure that the stepping-stones are

Right: Purple Loosestrife will grow over a metre tall with huge purple-spiked flowers – a paradise for insects.

Below: Great Willowherb is another wetland giant growing well over a metre tall. A spectacular addition to your pond edge or wetland.

Right: Meadowsweet is a common plant of marshes, wet woods and lakes and is a great plant for shady edges of your wetland.

smooth on the underside and embedded on a thick layer of soil to prevent them tearing the lining when you walk on them. The wettest part of the pond edge needs to be left so that it grades into a wildflower meadow. By keeping the water level high, grasses will be prevented from taking over. Cut the wetland plants every two to five years to stop scrub from invading. Carefully remove any seedling bushes or tree saplings by hand.

PLANTING GUIDE – WETLAND AND POND-EDGE PLANTS

Species	Plant height (cm)	Flower type and colour	When they flower	Where to plant them	Notes
Bugle (*Ajuga reptans*)	10-15	Deep blue	Apr-June	Partial shade	Great for providing colour in a shaded area.
Common Valerian (*Valeriana officinalis*)	30-120	Pink	June-July	Sun, partial or full shade	From the water's edge to the edge of a meadow
Creeping-Jenny (*Lysimachia nummularia*)	<10, sprawling	Yellow	May-Aug	Sun	Like a horizontal Yellow Loose-strife, this provides good ground cover.
Cuckooflower (*Cardamine pratensis*)	30-60	Pale pink	Apr-June	Sun or partial shade	Delicate flower to add early colour to a marsh or meadow.
Devil's-bit Scabious (*Succisa pratensis*)	60-110	Lilac-blue or purple	July-Oct	Partial shade	Great architectural plant that provides autumn food for birds.
Fritillary (*Fritillaria melagris*)	20-40	Pink, mottled	Mar-May	Sun	Its bulbs can be used to link a wildflower meadow to a marsh.
Great Willowherb (*Epilobium hirsutum*)	120	Pink spikes	July-Aug	Sun or partial shade	Will take care of itself and establish really quickly.
Hemp-agrimony (*Eupatorium cannabinum*)	30-120	Pink	July-Sept	Sun, partial or full shade	Flowers not exciting visually. Very attractive to insects, especially moths.
Lesser Celandine (*Ranunculus ficaria*)	5-25	Yellow	Mar-May	Partial to full shade	Great for providing early colour.
Marsh Cinquefoil (*Potentilla palustris*)	10-45	Pinkish-purple	June-July	Sun or partial shade	Good for an acid soil.
Marsh Marigold or Kingcup (*Caltha palustris*)	30-40	Yellow	Mar-May	Sun, partial or full shade	Great anywhere for early spring colour.
Meadow Buttercup (*Ranunculus acris*)	10-30	Yellow	June-Oct	Sun or partial shade	Good even if there is a bit of trampling or grazing.
Meadowsweet (*Filipendula ulmaria*)	60-120	White	June-Sept	Sun or partial shade	Great for all types of insect. Provides cover for small mammals.
Purple Loosestrife (*Lythrum salicaria*)	60-120	Huge purple spikes	June-Aug	Sun or partial shade	A purple paradise for insects.
Ragged Robin (*Lychnis flos-cuculi*)	30-50	Rose-red	May-Aug	Sun or partial shade	Can be cut, so is good for a summer meadow.
Yellow Loosestrife (*Lysimachia vulgaris*)	60-150	Many, yellow	July-Aug	Sun or partial shade	Great display of bold colour throughout the summer; butterflies and bees love it.

Wildlife in Focus

You can learn a lot about ecology by watching the miniature wildlife ecosystem in your pond. The relationships between the animals and plants in a pond are fascinating and quite easy to study.

Below: *A food web consists of several chains of organisms dependent on one another for supply of food, e.g. tadpoles eat plants and in turn newts eat tadpoles.*

Food webs

Understanding the interactions within a pond leads to an understanding of how a pond should be managed. Observe the food chains and webs, and note how the energy from dead plants and animals is recycled by other, usually microscopic creatures. At the bottom of the chain are tiny and often beautiful aquatic plants, such as

diatoms, which can be seen only with a good microscope. Sometimes, pond-water goes green because algae have got out of control. The best solution is to encourage the animals that feed on algae, such as the pond owner's best friends, the water fleas. When a pond looks slimy, this is also due to algae: those that grow in groups, with so many individuals that the colonies look like large, straggling plants. These filamentous

A typical pond's food web

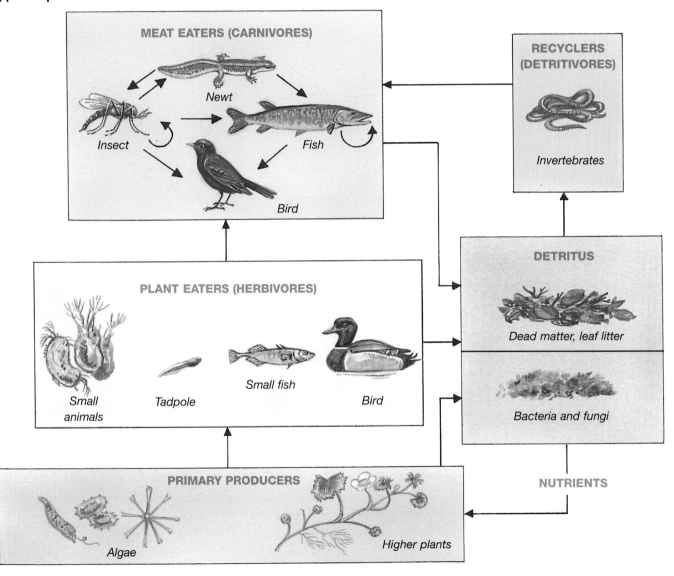

MEAT EATERS (CARNIVORES)

Newt

Insect

Fish

Bird

RECYCLERS (DETRITIVORES)

Invertebrates

PLANT EATERS (HERBIVORES)

Small animals

Tadpole

Small fish

Bird

DETRITUS

Dead matter, leaf litter

Bacteria and fungi

PRIMARY PRODUCERS

NUTRIENTS

Algae

Higher plants

Slice of life in a typical wildlife pond

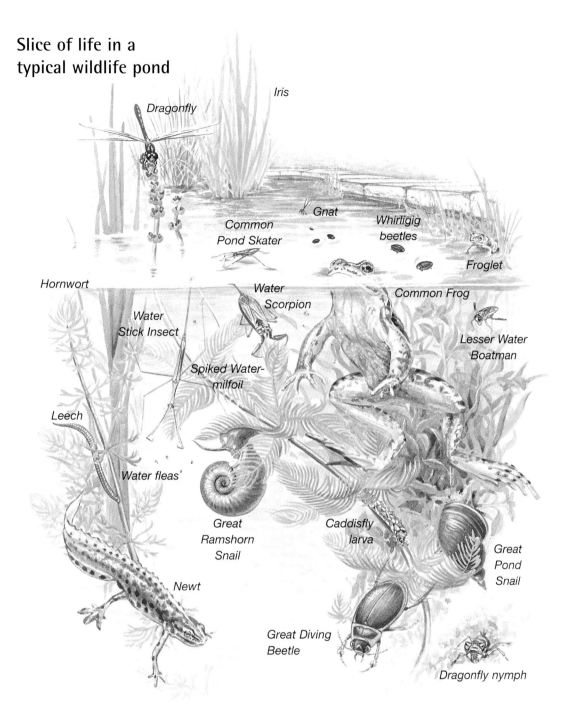

Iris

Dragonfly

Gnat

Common
Pond Skater

Whirligig
beetles

Froglet

Hornwort

Water
Scorpion

Common Frog

Water
Stick Insect

Lesser Water
Boatman

Spiked Water-
milfoil

Leech

Water fleas

Great
Ramshorn
Snail

Caddisfly
larva

Great
Pond
Snail

Newt

Great Diving
Beetle

Dragonfly nymph

Left: *The variety of life found in even small ponds is astounding. Predatory diving beetles hunt in the weeds and Water Scorpions wait to ambush their prey. Pond snails graze on algae and a variety of invertebrates scuttle about, cleaning up the dead and decaying plants.*

algae include *Spirogyra* and *Cladophora*, both of which are commonly found in garden ponds (see page 37). They are grazed by pond snails and other plant-eating animals.

Freshwater Shrimps, water fleas and other small insects form food for small fish and bigger insects, such as the voracious dragonfly nymphs. In their turn, these larger insects are eaten by larger fish. On land, vertebrates are usually the predators of invertebrates, but in ponds things are different. Large water beetle larvae or dragonfly nymphs frequently eat small fish or frog and toad tadpoles.

When small green plants and animals die, they are chopped up and eaten by those animals, known as detritivores, that feed on dead material. The small bits of matter that remain, called detritus, are broken down by bacteria and their nutrients go back to feed the small plants.

Nothing in a pond is wasted, and every organism forms part of the food web. Management, or interference, is necessary only when the natural balance is upset.

On the following pages are a selection of animals that may live in and around your pond along with details on how to attract them.

Bugs

Water bugs are bizarre, beautiful and brilliant. Some go hunting for their prey, while others merely sit on the water surface, hide amongst pond plants or under rocks in the pond, and ambush their prey. Some help to clean up the pond, feeding on dead and decaying plants, while others are herbivores, eating pondweed or helping to clear the pond of algae.

There are hundreds of water bugs to choose from, but my favourites are the predators. No horror film could produce more merciless or grisly predators. The Water Scorpion and Water Stick Insect look as if they would inject poisonous venom, but their seemingly lethal spikes are merely breathing tubes. Their huge pincers are, however, every bit as menacing as they look. A Common Pond Skater does not look menacing as

Above: *A monster in waiting – Water Scorpions ambush their unsuspecting prey and suck the life out of them, literally.*

it glides gracefully across the water surface, but this is an illusion, for it stabs its prey and sucks its insides out – a truly unpleasant way to go, even for a fly.

ATTRACTING BUGS TO YOUR POND

If you want lots of bug life you need plenty of different types of plants. Tall emergent plants allow the nymphs to clamber out as they emerge into adults. Many bugs lay their eggs into the stems of underwater plants so include some submerged plants in your pond.

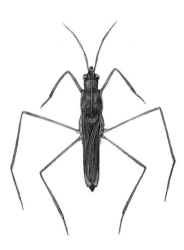

The **Common Pond Skater** (*Gerris lacustris*) is aptly named, since water-repellent hairs on their legs allow them to glide across the surface, just like skaters on ice.

Detecting insects on the water's surface both by vibration and by sight, they use their two hind legs as rudders, their middle legs as oars to propel them towards the struggling insect, and their two front legs to grab it. Like many true bugs, they do not have jaws, but instead have a pointed mouth called a rostrum, which contains deadly needle-like stylets. Once the prey is grabbed, the pond skater stabs with its stylets and sucks out its victim's insides.

The adults overwinter in sheltered places away from the water and return to the pond in spring to lay their eggs during May.

Length 10mm (up to 18mm).

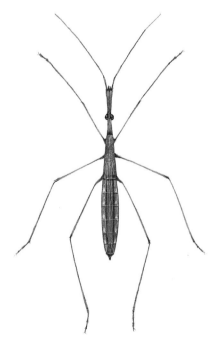

The **Water Measurer** (*Hydrometra stagnorum*) is another deadly predator that detects its prey through vibration, as it walks slowly on the water from plant to plant. It does not catch insects that land on the water's surface, but instead spears its prey through the surface.

The adults overwinter in the pond and pair in the spring, when the female sticks her long seed-like eggs to plant stems at the water surface.

Length 11mm (up to 15mm).

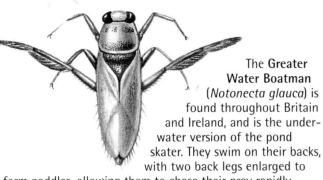

The **Greater Water Boatman** (*Notonecta glauca*) is found throughout Britain and Ireland, and is the underwater version of the pond skater. They swim on their backs, with two back legs enlarged to form paddles, allowing them to chase their prey rapidly through the water. Their prey, which is often much larger than themselves, is grabbed with their two forelegs, then stabbed and injected with toxic saliva. If you pick one up, it can inject that toxin into you; this stings like a very hard pinprick, but the effect doesn't last.

Adult water boatmen can fly, and are often one of the first predators to colonize a new pond. The adults mate from midwinter onwards, and the eggs are laid from as early as February, into the stems of water plants. The nymphs take about 8–10 weeks to mature.

Length 16mm.

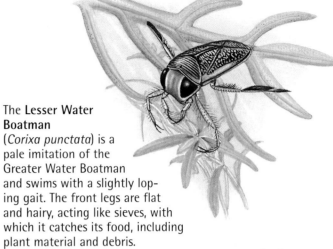

The **Lesser Water Boatman** (*Corixa punctata*) is a pale imitation of the Greater Water Boatman and swims with a slightly loping gait. The front legs are flat and hairy, acting like sieves, with which it catches its food, including plant material and debris.

It is a capable flier, though not so vigorous as the Greater Water Boatman. The males court the females by rubbing their hair patches on the inside of their front legs against the side of their 'beaks'. The females lay eggs on water plants from January to March.

Length up to 12mm.

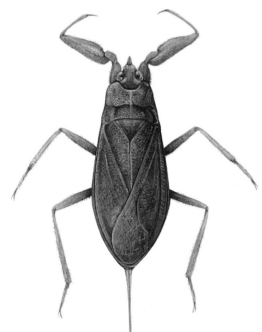

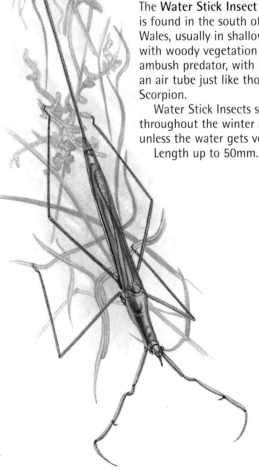

The **Water Stick Insect** (*Ranatra linearis*) is found in the south of England and Wales, usually in shallow water in ponds with woody vegetation and litter. It is an ambush predator, with huge pincers and an air tube just like those of the Water Scorpion.

Water Stick Insects stay in the pond throughout the winter and remain active unless the water gets very cold.

Length up to 50mm.

The **Water Scorpion** (*Nepa cinerea*) is found in weedy ponds and shallow lakes throughout Britain except for northern Scotland. It has a long tail that looks like the sting of a land-living scorpion, but is in fact a breathing tube, which penetrates the water.

It is one of nature's great imitators, ambushing its prey whilst pretending to be a leaf. It grabs small animals with its enormous pincers, preying especially upon tadpoles and small fish. It rarely swims, but sometimes walks along the bottom of the pond.

Length 20mm (tail measuring 8mm).

The **Water Cricket** (*Velia caprai*) is a tiny predator that lives on the water surface, usually on a pond with a slight flow of water. It locates prey by sight and by detecting ripples in the water surface, just like a miniature pond skater.

Length 6mm.

Beetles, spiders and flies

The sleek and shiny beetles are some of the most beautiful of pond insects, and are great fun to watch. Whirligig beetles whiz around the surface in groups, seemingly involved in an insect country-dance. All this grace belies their true nature: they are scavengers, searching for dead insects and dead fish. If whirligig beetles are the vultures of the pond world, then diving beetles are the big cats and the Great Diving Beetle is the tiger. Great Diving Beetles are huge predators, and if you see one flying towards you – duck!

Water Spiders look really frightening, as they glisten like metallic monsters. It is all an illusion, the shiny metallic appearance being caused by a bubble of air trapped around the hairs on their bodies, allowing this air-breathing spider to hunt in the water.

Last but not least are the flies, ranging from the elegant mayflies, with their transparent wings and delicate bodies, to the stocky and secretive stoneflies and caddisflies, with their wonderfully diverse larvae. Caddisfly larvae come with or without cases, which are their mobile homes, built out of small stones, sticks or gravel. Different species use different materials and the cases all differ in microscopic details. The moth-like adults hide amongst vegetation during the day and become active and fly at dusk.

Many true flies (*Diptera*) lay their eggs in water, including those most unpleasant of water dwellers, the blood-sucking mosquitoes and gnats. In fact, it is only the female mosquito that drinks blood, as she needs the energy to produce her eggs; the males are harmless and feed on plant nectar.

Above: *Mosquito maggots are filter-feeding larvae, which dangle below the water's surface.*

Whirligig beetles (Family *Gyrinidae*) are small, shiny, black beetles that have the habit of gyrating in groups on the surface of ponds and slow-moving water. When disturbed, they dive rapidly down into the pond. The commonest species is *Gyrinus marinus*, which is found on open water over most of Britain. They are active by day from spring to autumn, feeding on dead animals on the water surface. They have two pairs of eyes, for seeing both above and below the water surface. Their eggs are laid on submerged plants, and the larvae stay on the bottom of the pond until they are nearly full-grown. Length 6–7mm.

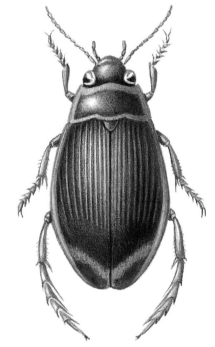

The **Great Diving Beetle** (*Dytiscus marginalis*) is one of the most spectacular of our pond insects. Both adults and larvae hunt in water and will eat anything that they can catch. The adults can fly. The larvae grow to a huge 50mm and have sickle-shaped pincers, with which they puncture and suck their prey, especially tadpoles, and are even more voracious than the adults.
Length 27mm (larvae 50mm).

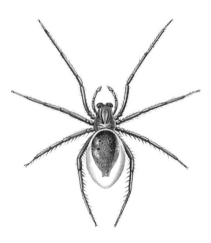

All spiders are air breathers, but the **Water Spider** (*Argyroneta aquatica*) has a remarkable trick: it builds a diving bell by trapping air in a web spun amongst pond plants. It visits the surface and collects air between the hairs on its abdomen, releasing this into their diving bell by stroking the hairs with its back legs. It lives in this bell, which it leaves only to hunt for insect larvae and pond skaters, its main prey.

A Water Spider will often spend the winter sealed inside an old snail shell.
Length 10mm.

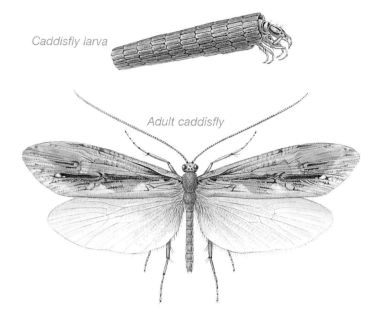

Caddisfly larva

Adult caddisfly

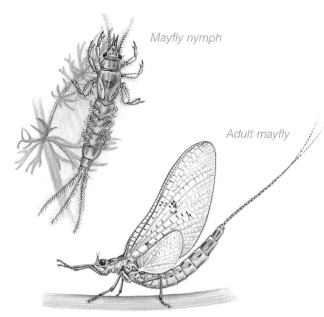

Mayfly nymph

Adult mayfly

There are nearly 200 species of **caddisflies** (*Trichoptera*), and their larvae all live in water. Some caddisfly larvae swim around without cases: they usually have a dark head and a paler body, with two small hooks at the end of their tail. Most species, however, make camouflaged cases to protect themselves from predators and to allow them to ambush their prey. Cased caddis larvae stick their chosen material to their bodies by winding sticky thread around themselves. As they grow, new bits are added to the head end. Different species live in different cases, some made of sand or small stones, others of pieces of leaf or wood. They all crawl along carrying their homes with them.

The moth-like adult caddisflies rest amongst vegetation during the day, flying mostly at dusk.

Wingspan up to 64mm (cased larvae up to 55mm).

Adult **mayflies** (*Ephemeroptera*) live for very short periods, some species for only a few hours, and do not feed, simply emerging in summer from the water to breed.

All mayfly nymphs have three tails; the adults may have two or three tails, but their forewings are always larger than their hindwings.

Adult **stoneflies** (*Plecoptera*) have two long, slender antennae, two tail filaments and four wings all of about equal size. The larvae of most species live in rivers, but some occur in ponds. The nymphs also have two tails; they cannot swim, but merely crawl on the bottom. Some species have gills, but they are never located on the sides of the abdomen (as they are on mayflies).

Some species are recyclers, feeding on fallen leaves, but others are predators.

Length 20mm.

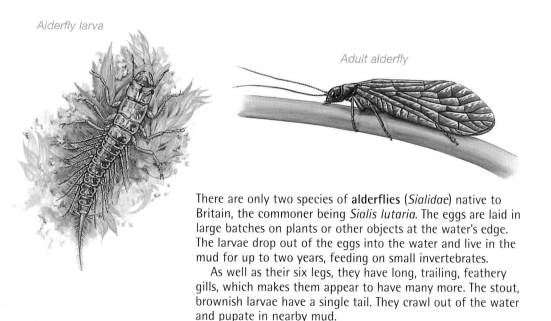

Alderfly larva

Adult alderfly

There are only two species of **alderflies** (*Sialidae*) native to Britain, the commoner being *Sialis lutaria*. The eggs are laid in large batches on plants or other objects at the water's edge. The larvae drop out of the eggs into the water and live in the mud for up to two years, feeding on small invertebrates.

As well as their six legs, they have long, trailing, feathery gills, which makes them appear to have many more. The stout, brownish larvae have a single tail. They crawl out of the water and pupate in nearby mud.

Length 18mm (larvae up to 40mm).

ATTRACTING BEETLES TO YOUR POND

Many beetles are predators. To attract them to your pond you need to attract lots of other insects. Shallow plant-filled margins are great places for beetles to hunt. Many species need mud to crawl on to, so leave some mud exposed.

57

Fleas, lice and snails

Fleas, lice and snails would probably not be welcome visitors to your house or even your garden, but you do need them in your pond. Actually, what you need are plenty of water fleas, hoglice and pond snails.

Above: *Not quite large enough for your barbecue, Freshwater Shrimps are welcome in your pond as they recycle nutrients.*

Water fleas are not fleas at all, but belong to the same group as crabs: the crustaceans. There are many species, all of them important in a pond, as they form a vital link in the food chain between plants and larger predatory insects. They got the name water flea from the way that they zip around in the water in jerky, apparently haphazard movements. In late spring and early summer, they can occur in vast numbers, and are able to consume huge quantities of algae. If there are too many fish, water flea numbers become depleted, algae grow uncontrolled, and the pond can end up looking like pea soup. Thus, water fleas are wonderful!

Hoglice are among nature's recyclers (detritivores), acting as well as looking like underwater woodlice. They break up dead leaves into smaller, more digestible bits that can then be consumed by other organisms.

Water snails are among the best grazing animals in ponds. Some munch their way through aquatic plants, but many simply graze the algae off the surface of the higher plants, so are the pond owner's friends. Snails: gardeners' friends? That really is a turn-up!

ATTRACTING FLEAS & LICE TO YOUR POND

Hoglice and water fleas will colonize almost any open water with plants. To keep plenty of hoglice, leave some dead plant material in the pond. For water fleas, make sure there aren't too many fish and do not use filters or chemicals.

There are many species of **water flea**. The ones most commonly seen in ponds belong to the genus *Daphnia*. Water fleas get eaten by lots of insects and by fish. In response to the presence of predators, some water fleas develop spines on their body.

Many species of water fleas, and other tiny animals called copepods, are often sold as fish food. Under difficult circumstances, such as a drying pond or in cold weather, water fleas produce thick-shelled eggs, which can lie dormant for several years, surviving desiccation. Since some water fleas have filaments designed to stick to birds' feathers and others are simply light enough to be carried by the wind, they are often among the first natural colonizers of a new pond.
Length 0.2–10mm.

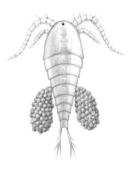

With its single eye, the **Cyclops** looks even more alien than its crustacean relatives. It is one of the easiest pond creatures to see even with the naked eye.

The females carry the eggs in two clusters like large panniers on their sides. It is a fast swimmer, which you will find out if you try to catch it with a pipette.
Length 2–5mm.

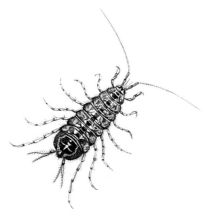

Hoglice (*Asellus*) are crustaceans and are among the most common invertebrates in ponds, which is a good thing, since we would be knee-deep in litter without them. They are greyish-brown, flat, look just like woodlice, and crawl rather than swim. The females are larger than the males and often carry eggs or young in a brood pouch under the abdomen. The most frequent species is *Asellus aquaticus*.
Length up to 20mm.

Freshwater Shrimps (*Gammaridae*) are much smaller than the marine shrimps found on barbecues. They swim quickly, on their sides, and often appear to shoot off in random directions. They can be incredibly common, especially in ponds with fallen leaves, and form an essential link in the food chain, recycling the nutrients in decaying plants and providing food for many predatory bugs. Their colour varies from reddish to grey. *Gammarus pulex* is the most common species, found throughout the UK.
Length up to 30mm (but usually much smaller).

There are two main types of **pond snails**: those with lids (operculate snails) and those without lids (pulmonate snails). The operculate snails have spirally-coiled shells and are able to retract into these, closing the entrance with a lid (operculum). Those most commonly found in ponds are all pulmonates, including pond snails (*Lymnaeidae*), bladder snails (*Physidae*) and ramshorn snails (*Planorbidae*).

All these snails are vegetarian, grazing on plants or on the algae that cover the plants, rocks and mud in the bottom of the pond.

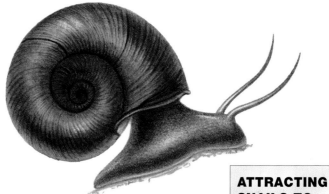

In areas of hard water, the **Great Pond Snail** (*Limnaea stagnalis*) is the commonest of the water snails in ponds, ditches and lakes. These aquatic 'mowers' of algae and weed, lay their eggs in jellied masses best found under the leaves of lily pads.
Length up to 50mm.

Ramshorn snails do not have pointed shells, but are coiled into a flat disc. The two commonest ramshorn snails are the **Great Ramshorn Snail** (*Planorbis corneus*) and the Common Ramshorn Snail (*P. planorbis*). Both contain red blood a bit like ours, but one form has a dark pigment that masks this, while another seems to lack this pigment and has a body and foot that is quite literally 'blood red'.
Length 18–25mm.

ATTRACTING SNAILS TO YOUR POND

Snails have a remarkable ability to find their way into your pond. If you want to ensure that they stay, make sure there are plenty of plants with floating leaves and underwater plants to provide food and habitat for them and their prey.

Dragonflies and damselflies

Mouthparts

Gills

Left: *In your pond, damselfly nymphs breathe using gills at the tip of their abdomen, which look like three feathers sticking out.*

One of the most awe-inspiring sites in any garden pond is a dragonfly or damselfly nymph catching its prey. Their lower jaw has pincer-like extensions called a mask and they shoot this out to catch their prey. They are voracious predators hunting down prey much larger than themselves, even catching small fish and amphibians.

Above the water the adults are equally fearsome as they hunt for flying insects. There are two main types of dragonfly: the typical or true dragonflies and the damselflies. Both types of dragonfly hunt by sight. True dragonflies are swift, agile fliers catching prey on the wing. Damselflies are smaller and have a rather weak-looking fluttery flight, usually catching their prey amongst vegetation.

Damselflies have long, thin abdomens and they usually hold their wings closed when at rest, unlike dragonflies, which hold their wings out when resting. Damselflies mate resting on plants, while dragonflies mate whilst flying.

There are three types of true dragonflies named after their method of chasing and catching prey: hawkers, chasers and darters. Hawkers are fast, powerful and agile fliers and show patrolling behaviour around their territory, often flying backwards and forwards, hence the name hawkers. Chaser dragonfly males maintain territories near water by chasing away strange males. They have fatter bodies than the other dragonflies. Darters have a habit of darting out from perches to grab unsuspecting prey.

Damselflies

The **Emerald Damselfly** (*Lestes sponsa*) is a small metallic blue-green or green-bodied damselfly, with dull blue eyes on the males. This is a likely visitor to your pond in most of Britain and Ireland. The female is usually duller, more bronze-green with a thicker body than the male. The adults fly from late June to September, though they rarely leave the cover of vegetation. Length 38mm.

A common sight almost everywhere in the British Isles from late April to September is the **Large Red Damselfly** (*Pyrrhosoma nymphula*). It has large black legs and the males have red eyes. The adults of both sexes are generally yellow at first, growing gradually redder. Length 36mm.

The **Blue-tailed Damselfly** (*Ischnura elegans*) is one of the commonest damselflies in Britain and Ireland, and is likely to be one of the first damselflies to colonize your pond. The females are rather variable in their colour patterns. The adults fly from early May to early September near or over plants at the edge of water. Length 31mm.

Hawker dragonflies

The **Common Hawker** (*Aeshna juncea*) is the most widespread of the hawkers. The mature male has blue eyes and large blue markings with smaller yellow markings along the abdomen. The female has mostly yellow marking and yellow-green eyes. Both males and females have golden-yellow leading edges to the wings. The Common Hawker is most common in the north and west, flying by day from late June to October. Length 74mm.

The **Golden-ringed Dragonfly** (*Cordulegaster boltoni*) is one of the largest dragonflies in Britain. Unlike most other dragonflies, the male and female are very similar. The body is black with yellow stripes, hence the name golden-ringed. They are common in the south and west of England, flying from early June to August. Length 74mm.

The **Emperor Dragonfly** (*Anax imperator*) is the largest British hawker dragonfly (wingspan up to 100mm). The adults may be seen patrolling and hunting in the sunshine and towards night-fall from late May to August around ponds and lakes in many parts of England; but they are common in the south-east only and are never found in Scotland. They prey upon smaller dragon-flies and many other insects. Length 78mm.

Chaser and darter dragonflies

The **Four-spotted Chaser** (*Libellula quadri-maculata*) is the largest of the family and is often seen in massive numbers on migration in northern Europe. The sexes are alike, both having two spots on each wing and black patches on the base of the hind wings. It is widespread, though rare in some parts of Scotland and northern England. The adults are on the wing from May to mid August, near stagnant or slow-moving water, but they may be seen flying swiftly along city streets when on migration. Length 43mm.

The **Broad-bodied Chaser** (*Libellula depressa*) is another migrant dragonfly that breeds in ponds in southern Britain. Both sexes have very broad, flattened abdomens – the mature adult males are blue and the young males and females are brown. They fly by day from early May to August in much the same habitats as Four-spotted Chaser, but rarely breed north of Lancashire and Yorkshire or in Ireland. Length 44mm.

The **Common Darter** (*Sympetrum striolatum*) is a medium-sized dragonfly with slender abdomen. They are often found far from water, swarming in grassy fields or along paths from mid June to late October. They often migrate in great swarms. You are most likely to see this if you live in the south of England, but it is found throughout the British Isles. Length 37mm.

Below: *One of the earliest visitors to your pond, Common Frogs are usually 60–100mm long when fully grown.*

Amphibians

To many people, frogs, toads and newts are pond life. During the breeding season, frogs and toads can be the most obvious and noisy inhabitants of a garden pond, their arrival heralding the start of spring.

There are six amphibian species that are commonly held to be native in the United Kingdom: three newts, two toads and one frog. The Natterjack Toad (*Bufo calamita*) is rare and protected, breeding in only a few places, mostly on coastal sand dunes and the occasional inland heath. Common Toads (*Bufo bufo*), on the other hand, may be found in many larger gardens, while Common Frogs (*Rana temporaria*), Smooth (*Triturus vulgaris*), Palmate (*T. helveticus*) and Great Crested Newts (*T. cristatus*) can be found in even the smallest ponds.

The word amphibian describes their life style: *amphi bios* means double life. All these species have adults that live mainly on land, but which return to water to breed. The eggs are laid in water and hatch into tadpoles, which later undergo a metamorphosis into tiny miniatures of the adults and emerge from the water to begin their life as mainly land-living animals.

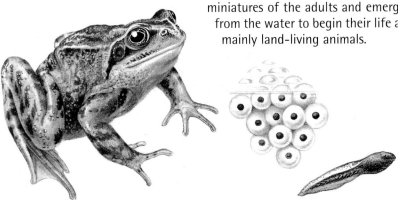

Fantastic frogs

The first amphibians to appear at a pond in spring are usually Common Frogs. As with other amphibians, the cue to emerge from hibernation is a combination of day length and temperature. In the south of England, frogs may be active in sheltered ponds as early as January, whilst in the north of Scotland they may not appear until March. Common Frogs are relatively short lived, rarely achieving an age of five years.

Frog breeding is a rather frantic affair as the males jump on the back of the first female that they can grab, and in the absence of a female will grab another male. Once they do have a female, the pair swims together towards the shallows, with the male grasping the female. This courtship swim is called amplexus. Clumps of Common Frog eggs (frog spawn) are laid in shallow water at the edge of ponds, where it will be warmer and the tadpoles will develop quicker than in colder deep water.

The tadpoles spend up to 12 weeks in the water before they are fully metamorphosed into miniature frogs. These froglets can be seen in the damp grass around the pond shortly after rain in May and June, but it will take two to four years for them to reach maturity and return to the pond to breed.

After the breeding season, the adult frogs may move away from the pond, though they will return from time to time to rehydrate. They feed on all sorts of small, moving invertebrates, such as slugs, snails, caterpillars, worms, flies and beetles. A frog catches its prey by flicking out its long sticky tongue and pulling the prey back into its gaping mouth.

In the 1980s, a small population of unusual Pool Frogs (*Rana lessonae*) were discovered. They looked and sounded different to Pool Frogs found in the rest of Europe and looked more like isolated populations found in Scandinavia. After much research, including analysis of fossil bones, DNA and frog-calling 'dialects' it appears that these Pool Frogs were different and were probably native to the UK.

Unfortunately, this unique population became extinct shortly after they were discovered. However, it is not all bad news. Now that it is known that these beautiful green frogs were probably native, various conservation agencies are attempting to re-introduce Pool Frogs from their nearest relatives in Scandinavia.

Left: *Common Frog spawn is laid in clumps of hundreds or thousands of eggs. Not many survive to become froglets due to a variety of predators.*

Terrific toads

I have a very soft spot for Common Toads, since I spent several years studying them. They are not the easiest of animals to study: they are coloured to fit in with their background and spend most of their time hiding. There were many drizzly evenings when I wished that I had chosen to study the behaviour of sun-loving butterflies for my PhD, instead of a species that is largely nocturnal and becomes active only when it is warm and wet.

Common Toads are more terrestrial and nomadic than frogs and will wander as far as 1km from their breeding site. They can live for up to 40 years, but most survive for only six or seven years. The Common Toad is our largest native amphibian.

One of the most common questions is 'What is the difference between a toad and a frog?' The answer is that there is no single difference, but the British species do demonstrate some of the general trends. Frogs tend to be more aquatic and to leap to escape predators. Toads tend to be more terrestrial and those in the genus *Bufo* (which includes both our native toads) can leap, but have another more-deadly deterrent. Toads secrete a toxin from their glands, situated behind their eyes. This toxin is surprisingly powerful: just 1g could kill a human being. There is no need to worry, however, as it would require hundreds if not thousands of toads to produce so much toxin. People and their household pets are safe; although a dog or cat silly enough to try to eat a toad may regret the experience, it will suffer no greater effect than if you or I ate something too spicy or too hot.

Frogs leap, so tend to have longer and more prominent hind limbs, whereas toads have shorter legs, better suited for scurrying. Toads also have mucus glands all over their bodies, so appear warty. Despite the toads' toxic defence, Hedgehogs and Otters, as well as several species of large bird, eat toads, and many other species kill them, but only rarely eat them. Rats are especially adept at catching toads, often killing many hundreds during the breeding season, peeling off the poisonous skin before eating them.

Toads overwinter in sites that will protect them from frosts and predators – such as dry-stone walls, log or litter piles, compost heaps or animal burrows. In spring, they return to breed, usually in the pond where they were bred. They

often gather in even greater numbers than do frogs, and on warm, wet spring nights, it is possible to see thousands of toads walking to some breeding sites.

There is even more competition between male toads for female toads than there is in the case of frogs. Most females are leapt upon by the first male that they encounter, and very few females will reach the water without a male clinging to their backs. Larger males frequently usurp smaller males. The female toads are older and larger than the males. The competition for mates can be so intense that the females may drown under a clump of males all trying to mate with her.

The strings of black eggs are arranged in a double row and are then tangled around pondweed. Common Toad tadpoles take two or three months to develop before they metamorphose, and the toadlets emerge from the pond in June or July.

Adult Common Toads have a similar diet to Common Frogs, including beetles, slugs and worms. They sometimes return year after year to the same area to feed.

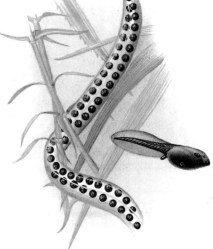

Above: *Common Toads mating – each female lays about 600–4,000 eggs, the largest females laying the most eggs. Toad courtship is hardly a romantic affair; there can be so many males trying to mate with a single female that females occasionally drown.*

Below: *Common Toads are usually 80–150mm in length. The tadpoles are protected by the same toxins as the adults, which make them distasteful to fish and other predators.*

Newts

The Great Crested Newt is by far the largest of our native species, reaching up to 170mm in length, and is rather flattened, with a very long tail. Unlike our other newts, it has granular skin, hence its alternative name of Warty Newt. These lumps are mucus glands, so Great Crested Newts always appear wet and velvety, even on dry land. As the name suggests, the male develops a huge ridged crest along his back in the breeding season, and the female develops a ridge down the centre of her back. Great Crested Newts take about three years to become sexually mature.

The Smooth Newt is typically smaller, about 110mm long, and resembles a less-flattened version of the Great Crested Newt. It is usually a dull yellow-brown colour, but during the breeding season the male develops a bright orange stripe on his belly.

The Palmate Newt is smallest of all, up to 100mm long when full grown, and is very dull looking in comparison with the other newts. The breeding male develops a unique short black filament at the end of his tail.

Newts are a little less fussy than toads and frogs about returning to their natal breeding sites, tending to move between ponds more often. Since Great Crested Newts often live in temporary ponds, some of which dry out in the summer, willingness to engage in site-switching is essential. A female Great Crested Newt lays 200–300 small (2mm), round eggs during April to July. The tadpoles spend four months in the water.

Smooth Newts lay 300–700 eggs, each one placed inside a carefully folded leaf. The female lays only two or three of her oval eggs per hour, so can take a week to deposit a batch before she goes off to mate with another male.

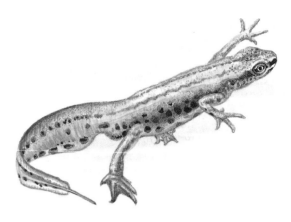

Above: *Palmate Newt males can be distinguished from the other newt species as they have a black filament at the end of their tails.*

The female Palmate Newt lays 300–400 eggs. The tadpoles of Smooth and Palmate Newts take only about 10–12 weeks to develop, with the newtlets metamorphosing during August. Palmate newtlets emerge as tiny 25mm replicas of the adults; Smooth newtlets are bigger, at up to 40mm; and Great Crested newtlets are the largest, at up to 70mm.

Great Crested Newt tadpoles are aggressive predators, feeding on just about anything, including small worms, insect larvae, frog and toad tadpoles and young fish. Smooth and Palmate Newt tadpoles are smaller, and their prey is also smaller, consisting of insect larvae and tadpoles. Adult Great Crested Newts are even more voracious and will even eat juvenile Great Crested Newts and water snails. Newt tadpoles are eaten by a wide range of predators, including water beetle larvae and minnows and sticklebacks.

Above: *Smooth Newts are our commonest newt. The orangey underparts become duller in winter.*

Below: *Great Crested Newts' courtship is an intricate affair. Male newts go to great lengths to woo the females.*

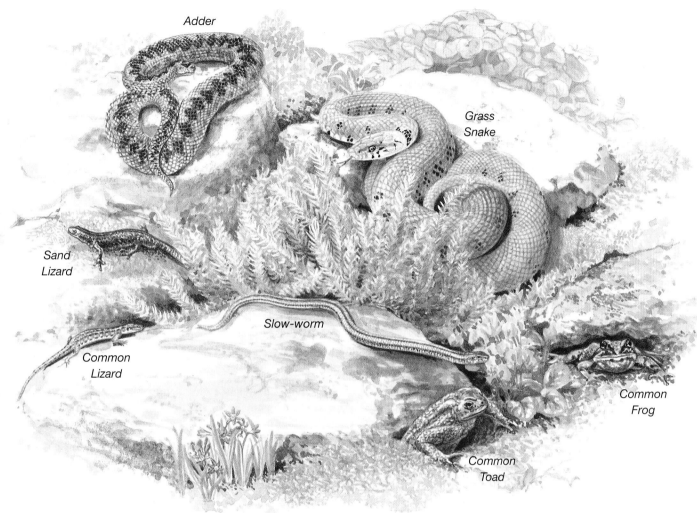

Adder

Grass Snake

Sand Lizard

Common Lizard

Slow-worm

Common Frog

Common Toad

Reptiles

While most reptiles need dry, warm sites in which to bask and warm up, and to breed and overwinter, they can also benefit from wetland. The combination of a rockery, a wetland, a compost heap and a log pile, (as described in *Fantastic Features* on page 32), is perfect, and provides habitat for lizards, including Slow-worms (*Anguis fragilis*).

Adders (*Vipera beris*) do occur naturally in wetlands, such as peat-bog areas, but are much more frequent in dry habitats. Only one native British reptile is a water and wetland specialist: the Grass Snake (*Natrix natrix*). It is easy to distinguish from other snakes by its distinctive yellow collar. Female Grass Snakes are larger than the males and can grow to over 1.5m in length, though the ones that visit garden ponds are usually juveniles or much smaller adults. If disturbed, a Grass Snake will retreat to hide in long grass or under a rock, a log, debris or any bit of cover. They are fantastic swimmers and may dive below the water, especially when threatened.

Grass Snakes can live for up to 25 years, but most live much shorter lives as they are usually killed and eaten by the larger predators, such as Otters, Red Foxes and Grey Herons.

A garden pond teaming with amphibians and their tadpoles is a favourite hunting ground for Grass Snakes. They come out of hibernation in early April, when the Common Toad breeding season is in full swing, and remain active until October. They mate in April and May, and the females lay clutches of 8–40 eggs in piles of rotting leaves (the compost heap is a favourite place) during June and July. The rotting causes the temperature to rise in the centre of the vegetation piles, and the eggs develop in these hot, moist conditions. The baby snakes – 15–20cm miniatures of the adults – hatch in late August or early September. It takes three or four years before these juveniles mature and breed, during which time they feed on tadpoles, newts, fish, earthworms and insects. Grass Snakes will bite people only if they are handled, and they are not venomous. If you disturb them, they may discharge a smelly fluid that will ruin your clothes.

Above: *All British reptiles may visit garden ponds, but Slow-worms and Grass Snakes are the most common visitors.*

ATTRACTING REPTILES TO YOUR POND

To attract reptiles you need various accessories for your pond. Reptiles need somewhere to overwinter, so provide log or rock piles as refuges. Compost heaps are ideal places for reptiles to breed.

Birds

Birds are attracted to ponds for drinking, bathing and feeding. Most garden birds will visit a pond from time to time, although the priorities are different for different species and at different times of the year. Watching a pond can provide constant entertainment as species come and go: little flocks of House Sparrows (*Passer domesticus*) boldly bathing and drinking, Starlings (*Sturnus vulgaris*) and Blackbirds (*Turdus merula*) splashing water everywhere. You could be lucky enough to see Goldfinches (*Carduelis carduelis*) dropping in for a sip, or a wagtail (*Motacilla*) bobbing and feeding on insect larvae and flies at the edge of your pond.

In the winter, birds need water to drink just as much as they need food, so if you maintain an ice-free area you will be helping them to survive the most difficult time of the year (see *De-icing frozen ponds* on page 72). You will also benefit, by seeing winter visitors such as Redwings (*Turdus iliacus*) and Siskins (*Carduelis spinus*), as well as resident birds such as Robins (*Erithacus rubecula*) and Bullfinches (*Pyrrhula pyrrhula*), at relatively close quarters.

Above: *A Blackbird may bathe in your pond, washing the dirt from its feathers.*

There are several bird species that are especially associated with water. If you live by a river or canal, you may catch a glimpse of iridescent blue as a Kingfisher (*Alcedo atthis*) flashes past. With its metallic blue and green upperparts and chestnut-red underparts, this is one of our most brightly coloured birds. Even tiny ponds can be visited by a Kingfisher or by a Grey Heron (*Ardea cinerea*) in search of fish or amphibians.

Large ponds with fringes of tall vegetation may attract Sedge Warblers (*Acrocephalus schoenobaenus*), Reed Buntings (*Emberiza schoeniclus*) or even Reed Warblers (*A. scirpaceus*). Only the largest ponds and lakes, with extensive areas of open water, will regularly attract ducks, geese and swans, Moorhens (*Gallinula chloropus*), Coots (*Fulica atra*), Little Grebes (*Tachybaptus ruficollis*) and Great Crested Grebes (*Podiceps cristatus*).

If you have a large pond or lake, water birds, such as Canada Geese (*Branda canadensis*), can increase the nutrients if they visit in large numbers. To stop large flocks of geese staying, make the surrounding habitat unsuitable. Since they need large areas of short grass or crops to feed, keep your pond away from your lawn. Large numbers of wildfowl will not settle on small, shallow ponds, so designing a series of wetlands rather than a large lake will prevent this problem.

Left: *Larger birds such as Woodpigeons may visit your pond to quench their thirst on a particularly hot summer's day.*

The **Robin** (*Erithacus rubecula*) is resident all year round, breeding in woodlands, parks and gardens. A keen singer, Robins will find a perch on which to sing and then proceed to out do the rest of the birds in the dawn chorus. Robins will benefit from your pond all year around.
Length 130–150mm.

The **Starling** (*Sturnus vulgaris*) is a common bird, often seen in large winter flocks over towns and cities. They breed prolifically and can be seen feeding in farmland, parks and gardens.
Often over-looked, starlings have iridescent green feathers and beautiful mottled colours.
Length 205–225mm.

House Sparrows
(*Passer domesticus*) are very familiar resident garden birds, and will visit your pond to drink. Winter males are duller than their summer counterparts.
Length 140–155mm.

The **Pied Wagtail** (*Motacilla alba*) is common in Britain and Ireland. These resident birds roost in large flocks during the winter. In the spring and summer they feed and breed often quite close to human activity.
Length 170–180mm.

Another resident, the **Bullfinch** (*Pyrrhula pyrrhula*) is fairly common, and can be seen in hedgerows, woodland edges and, particularly in winter and spring, in gardens. Although shy, they are fond of fruit tree buds and seeds so tempt them into your garden with a few apple, pear or cherry trees.
Length 140–150mm.

Mammals

Hedgehogs

The most likely mammalian visitor to a garden pond is a Hedgehog (*Erinaceus europaeus*). These short, rounded, unmistakable, prickly creatures have a snuffly charm all their own. They usually run away quickly from predators, or will roll into a ball, but are also quite capable swimmers.

Above: *Hedgehogs announce their arrival by snuffling and stomping through undergrowth. Don't be fooled by their cute appearance – they are excellent hunters.*

Hedgehogs are fearsome predators, eating not only invertebrates, but also small mammals and even snakes. They often come to drink at a pond, and also find it a great place to hunt for prey. They eat about 70g of animals every night, and will come to bowls of pet food or table scraps (but bread and milk makes them ill, so should not be provided). They are mainly nocturnal, but have diagnostic blackish droppings (containing remains of beetles and other insects), which may reveal their presence even if you don't see them.

Water Voles

Water Voles (*Arvicola terrestris*) used to be one of our commonest mammals, found along nearly all streams, rivers and canals. Unfortunately, poor habitat management has reduced their numbers, this decline being exacerbated by the dreaded American Mink. Small streams and ponds are one of the last refuges for Water Voles, though their habit of burrowing means they are very unlikely to frequent lined garden ponds.

They resemble large field voles, about 120–260mm in body length, with fur-covered tails and very rounded noses. They seldom stray far from water, occupying complex underground burrows, with at least one entrance below water level. They are vegetarians and leave lots of evidence of their presence, including burrow entrances, grazed lawns around these entrances, neat piles of cut grass stems at their feeding stations and piles of droppings known as latrines.

Bats

The Pipistrelle (*Pipistrellus pipistrellus*) is the most common, widely distributed bat in Britain, and is the one most likely to be seen in a garden. It frequently hunts low across stretches of water, fluttering untidily, and occasionally flying high above the surface before descending again.

Daubenton's Bat (*Myotis daubentoni*) is a medium-sized bat, about 40–50mm in length. It is always found close to water, and frequently hunts for its prey just above the water, so is sometimes known as the Water Bat. As well as

Left: *Water Voles were once a common sight on the waterways throughout the UK. Unfortunately, predation by American Mink and loss of habitat have reduced populations.*

being an agile flyer, it is a capable swimmer, able to take off from the water surface.

Many other bat species also hunt over water, including Whiskered Bat (*Myotis mystacinus*), Natterer's Bat (*Myotis nattereri*), and the rare Barbastelle Bat (*Barbastella barbastellus*).

Otters (and minks)

Otters (*Lutra lutra*) are very shy, and the chances of one visiting any but the largest garden situated close to a river is very slight; so, if you do get a visit from one, be extremely grateful. Once persecuted, these beautiful creatures are beginning to increase in numbers, helped by legal protection and conservation care.

Very well adapted for their semi-aquatic life, Otters have long, flattened bodies, with prominent whiskers on their rounded snouts, and tiny ears on the top of the head, so they can swim with their nose, ears and eyes out of the water. Fish form 90 per cent of their diet, but they will also take amphibians, small aquatic birds, crustaceans and molluscs. They are active mainly from dusk to dawn. Their presence is most often revealed by their special droppings, called spraints, placed on obvious signposts, such as rocks, in order to mark their territories.

Unfortunately, there is another mammal, looking very much like an Otter, that is more likely to appear at a garden pond: the American Mink (*Mustela vison*). American Minks have escaped or been deliberately released from mink farms and are voracious predators. They have driven Water Voles to the verge of extinction in many countries and are causing problems for ground-nesting birds and many other native species. The Mink can be distinguished from an Otter by its more-pointed face, bushier tail and more-jerky swimming action.

Foxes

Red Foxes (*Vulpes vulpes*) are often unseen nocturnal garden visitors, and are becoming more and more urban. They are active mostly at dusk and dawn. Their traditional prey is small mammals and Rabbits, but they are omnivores and will eat almost anything, including berries, beetles, other insects and worms. In urban areas, up to 60 per cent of their food comes from scavenging at compost heaps and dustbins.

Above: *Pipistrelles can often be seen feeding low over water. It is our smallest bat, with a wingspan of 200mm. Occasionally, they appear during the daytime, but more often at dusk.*

Below: *As our only wild dog species, Red Foxes are excellent hunters. They will come to feed on the other wildlife that is attracted to your pond, such as small mammals and beetles.*

A Year in the Life of a Pond

The ethos of good pond management is little and not-so-often. Throughout the year, there are always small tasks that can be done to keep your pond in perfect condition. In mid summer, however, just sit back, put your feet up, and watch the pond life go by. Bliss!

Spring
(March, April and May)

In spring and early summer, there is lots to see and do in the wildlife pond. The arrival of springtime is heralded by the chorus of frogs and shimmering balls of frog spawn at pond edges. Later, toads may arrive, making even more noise than the frogs. A torchlight visit at night will reveal their maximum activity. Indeed, everything starts to become active: plants bud and grow, and water fleas and other invertebrates become evident.

This sudden plant growth can cause problems, as duckweed and algae, such as blanket weed, may spread alarmingly. Remove excess duckweed by skimming the pond surface with a net, and blanket weed by twining it around a stick.

Marginal plants can be divided and replanted in early spring, which is also the best time to plant new aquatic plants, so that they have the whole summer to become established before the next winter's frosts. If you have planted flowering heathers around your pond, the dry stems should be clipped with shears in March.

Summer
(June, July and August)

On balmy summer days, take every opportunity to relax a little distance away from the pond, remain still and quiet, and just wait and watch to see what happens. Keep pond maintenance and disturbance to a bare minimum, as most invertebrates and other animals will be breeding. Insects become more active when it is warm, so look out for butterflies and dragonflies on a sunny day. Other good times to watch for

Left: *In spring, ponds become a riot of noise and colour, with flowering Marsh Marigolds and a chorus of frogs.*

Above: *Peacock Butterflies will visit ponds to feed on flowering pond plants – Purple Loosestrife is a butterfly bonanza.*

garden wildlife are in the twilight at dawn and at dusk, and just after a shower of rain.

On a balmy summer night, watching wildlife by torchlight can be an exciting introduction to nature for children. Similarly, pond dipping, with a small net on a long cane, provides a close-up view of wildlife, but needs to be done carefully to avoid undue disturbance.

In summer, many animals leave the pond: dragonflies and alderflies emerge, and tiny toadlets and froglets crawl onto the land. When these amphibians emerge, it is important not to mow the grass immediately around the pond and to be very careful when cutting elsewhere in the garden.

It may be necessary to top up the pond in hot summers, but the mud exposed by dropping water levels can be valuable to wildlife, so do not fill the pond to the top. Tap water may be quite rich in nutrients, so, if possible, collect and use rainwater instead.

Autumn
(September, October and November)

Many insect larvae will have emerged from the water and left the pond. Most plant growth starts to slow down, and most flowers will have set their seeds. The water level can be at its lowest in autumn, but autumn and winter rains will soon compensate for summer losses.

This is a good time for a little pond maintenance. Small amounts of silt can be cleared out, and reeds or other large plants should be removed or cut back if they have been growing

Right: *Lazy, hazy summer days are the best time for sitting and watching the variety of wildlife around your pond.*

too vigorously. Leaves from surrounding trees should be removed from the pond surface regularly, before they sink, rot and release unwelcome nutrients; add them to the compost heap. This is also a good time to fix any leaks that may have become apparent in the pond lining.

Winter
(December, January and February)

Winter is a tranquil time for your pond; a layer of snow on the water's surface is a pleasure to behold. Winter can, however, present a threat to pond survival. During long cold spells water in the shallow parts of the pond can freeze. This can threaten the survival of some species, and change the water chemistry of the pond. Oxygen diffuses into water from the air and is essential for pond life. Without oxygen, ponds become anoxic and many animals may die.

Frozen ponds can present a hazard to children and pets. The ice on ponds is rarely thick enough to walk on. Ensure everyone is aware of the dangers of falling through broken ice. Wildlife ponds are usually safer than ornamental ponds, as they are shallow and easy to get out of, even when frozen!

DE-ICING FROZEN PONDS

Open an air hole in the ice by holding a pan of hot water on the surface as soon as a continuous ice layer forms. Air holes should be opened every day during long freezing spells. These allow oxygen to diffuse into the water from the air and allow gases to escape from the pond. Banging holes in the ice is like an earthquake for the pond and may kill over-wintering wildlife. Never use salt or chemicals like antifreeze as these will kill wildlife and could permanently damage the water quality in your pond.

THE POND – MONTH BY MONTH

Month	Pondlife/Garden life	Garden tasks
January	Residents and winter visitors will come to drink and to feed, especially if you also have a regularly-stocked bird feeder.	Make holes if there is ice on the pond, to allow the water to 'breathe'. Put out wildlife food on a regular basis.
February	Frogs and toads begin to emerge from hibernation and may breed in southern counties of England. Catkins appear on willows.	Prune deciduous woody perennials and trim evergreen species. Lift and divide hardy perennials.
March	Pond plants start to grow. Frogs and toads mate and spawn. Lesser Celandine produces bright yellow flowers.	If you do not yet have one, create a pond. Build and erect a bat box. Clip flowering Heather (*Calluna vulgaris*). Divide and replant marginal and wetland plants.
April	Pond plants are growing strongly. Look for strings of toad spawn wound around pond plants. Beautiful bell-shaped flowers of Fritillaries appear.	Plant new water and wetland plants. If you do not already have one, create a marsh or bog garden.
May	Newts arrive in the pond and males attain breeding colour. Dragonflies appear: watch out for Broad-bodied Chasers fiercely defending their territories.	A good time to construct a rockery or rock bank to accompany your pond. Remove duckweed and blanket weed if necessary.
June	Tadpoles begin to metamorphose into adults, so catch some to watch as they develop legs. Ragged Robin flowers. Lots of insect life visible on sunny days. Look out for adult alderflies, caddisflies and damselflies.	Cut a spring-flowering meadow. Lift and divide spring bulbs from the wildflower meadow and rhizomes of Yellow Irises.
July	Bats may visit the pond to feed on emerging insects. Toadlets and froglets leave the pond. Many dragonflies and butterflies are on the wing.	Top up the pond, preferably with rainwater, if absolutely necessary. Clear out filamentous algae (blanket weed). Do a butterfly count.
August	Water boatmen, pond skaters and other surface dwellers will be visible. Adult newts may leave the pond. Frogs, especially juveniles, may return to the pond to rehydrate. Purple Loosestrife in full flower.	Top up the pond, if absolutely necessary. A good time for pond dipping.
September	Juvenile and adult birds will visit the pond to feed on insects as well as to drink. Downy Emerald Dragonfly may still be on the wing.	Collect seed from late-flowering plants. Cut the meadow for the last time in the year.
October	Some amphibians will make a small migration towards their overwintering sites: look out for them on warm wet nights. Watch out for frogs when lawn-mowing. Birds and even Red Foxes will come to scrump fallen apples.	Plant spring-flowering bulbs such as Bluebells and Snowdrops. Create winter habitat for overwintering insects, amphibians and reptiles. Remove some silt, if necessary, and remove excessive vegetation. Skim fallen leaves from the pond's surface.
November	Amphibians may still be active. Birds and many small mammals come to feed on berries.	Plant bulbs such as Fritillary and some lilies. Continue to remove leaves from the pond. Build a bird table.
December	Resident and wintering migrant birds will welcome a regularly-stocked bird feeder.	Make holes in ice on the pond. Feed birds. Coppice or pollard alders and willows. Build and erect nest boxes, ready for the spring.

Wonderful wetlands

Here are a few of our wonderful wetlands, to inspire you to build your own wildlife haven. Go along with a notebook and take notes, draw sketches and glean ideas.

Ainsdale Sand Dunes, near Southport, Lancashire
This large sand-dune system is one of my personal favourites. There is a lovely walk around the edge of the National Nature Reserve and through the local Nature Reserve. A series of shallow pools is home to Natterjack Toads, Smooth Newts and Great Crested Newts, and deeper pools host Common Frogs and Common Toads in huge numbers. Protected Sand Lizards are found in the dunes, and native Red Squirrels scamper in the fringing woodland. A very special place! Access away from public paths requires a permit from English Nature.

Ashleworth Ham, Worcestershire – Wildlife Trust
To visit this 40ha nature reserve in the flood plain of the Severn Vale near Ashleworth village, a local Wildlife Trust permit is needed. Ducks such as Wigeon and Teal can be seen in winter, and there are many beautiful flowers in spring and summer when the main floods have gone. Access may be prohibited in winter, but the birds can be viewed from hides.

Barn Elms, London – Wildfowl and Wetlands Trust (WWT)
The Wildfowl and Wetlands Trust and Thames Water have transformed old Victorian reservoirs into a 42ha award-winning wetland near Hammersmith Bridge in southwest London. The reserve is a Site of Special Scientific Interest (SSSI) for its overwintering wildfowl, and is noted for its 18 dragonfly species and a host of other wetland wonders. There is a purpose-built visitor centre – fun for all the family.

Brandon Marsh, Warwickshire – Wildlife Trust
This reserve, only 2km south-east of Coventry, is part of a former gravel extraction, now restored as a wetland, with reedbeds, wet woodland, grassland and many small pools. It is fantastic for birds and has a visitor centre, with good disabled access, and a sensory garden for the blind and visually impaired.

Castle Espie, Strangford Lough, south of Belfast, Northern Ireland
This site, 5km south of Comber, has great history and great wildlife. As well as all the expected birds, there are Otters, Badgers and Red Foxes. Magic!

Dartmoor National Park, Devon
With an area of 950 km² and over 950km of rights of way, this well-known, beautiful moorland contains natural wooded valleys and is renowned for bog vegetation such as Bog Pimpernel and Bog Asphodel.

Decoy Heath, near Silchester, Berkshire – Wildlife Trust
This 7ha Wildlife Trust Reserve has 23 species of breeding dragonfly, including the rare Downy Emerald and Brilliant Emerald Dragonflies. There are well-vegetated pools with native pond plants, such as Marsh Speedwell and Marsh Violet, and open heath, where there are Grass Snakes and Adders.

Llanelli Estuary, Carmarthenshire, Wales – WWT
Situated 6km east of Llanelli, this is one of the Wildfowl & Wetlands Trust's eight visitor centres. Its ponds, lakes and reedbeds host thousands of ducks, geese and swans, and there are breeding waders, Kingfishers and Short-eared Owls, as well as wildflowers, butterflies, dragonflies and other native wildlife.

Loch of Lowes, Dunkeld, Perthshire, Scotland – Wildlife Trust
This 134ha site, set in the uplands of Dunkeld, mostly comprises water managed by The Scottish Wildlife Trust. Observation hides with TV cameras allow wildlife to be watched up close without disturbance. Ospreys occur in summer, and there are Otters, interesting mosses and dragonflies. Fantastic! Dogs are not allowed.

Lymington Reedbeds, Hampshire – Wildlife Trust
This 35ha site, immediately east of Lymington, is one of the largest reedbeds on the South Coast. There is no public access to the reedbeds, but they can be viewed from footpaths and the adjacent road. As well as common marshland birds, there are Bearded Tits and Cetti's Warblers. In winter, you may hear a Water Rail's pig-like squeals.

Meres and Mosses, Cheshire
A series of holes, created during the last Ice Age, subsequently filled with water to become meres, and some then filled with vegetation to become floating or quaking bogs, known as mosses. One such site is the 12ha Hatchmere Delamere, a beautiful fen woodland with a wide range of wetland plants and animals.

Potteric Carr, Yorkshire – Wildlife Trust
This site, south-east of Doncaster, lies within an area of former fenland that was drained for agriculture, but then returned to its former condition as a result of mining subsidence. It constitutes the largest fen in South Yorkshire. Over 70 bird species breed, including Kingfisher, Long-eared Owl, Grasshopper, Reed and Sedge Warblers, and all three native woodpeckers. Its 19 species of dragonfly include Black-tailed Skimmer, Banded Demoiselle, Hairy Dragonfly and Ruddy Darter. Access is by permit only, and there is a charge.

Redgrave and Lopham Fen, Norfolk – Wildlife Trust
One of the most beautiful fens in England, this site was saved by intensive restoration. It is one of only two places in Britain where the impressive Raft Spider is found. The fens are grazed by beautiful wild Tarpan ponies, which roam wild amongst the reeds, helping to keep invading trees in check. Another plus: the visitor centre sells great cakes!

Welsh Wildlife Centre, Cardigan, Wales – Wildlife Trust
This 100ha reserve has 8km of footpaths that weave through woodland, meadow, reedbed and marsh near the beautiful river Teifi. There is an adventure playground for children, and a fantastic reserve restaurant that overlooks the second-largest reedbed in Wales. There is a chance of seeing an Otter or a Cetti's Warbler, as well as many more-common waterbirds, from the comfort of a chair. Even more fantastic are the Asian Water Buffaloes that graze the reserve.

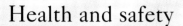

Health and safety

The risks associated with ponds can be minimized by careful planning and commonsense. The main risk that most people associate with ponds is drowning, but, according to data for 1997 from the Royal Society for the Prevention of Accidents (ROSPA), a total of only nine people drowned in ponds in that year (compared with 132 who drowned in rivers and streams, 35 in canals, and 26 in their own baths).

Wildlife ponds are designed with shallow sloping margins and shallow water, which greatly reduces the risk to everyone, except toddlers and small pets.

To keep safe in and around ponds and water bodies, follow the advice given by ROSPA. This is relevant to all water bodies, but particularly refers to those with public access.

- When working in or near deep water, always wear a life-jacket.
- Rivers and streams are prone to flood, so should be avoided after heavy rain.
- Steep and unstable banks should always be avoided.

Water can contain invisible hazardous substances that are dangerous or even lethal. The main bacteriological risk is Weil's Disease (*Leptospirosis*), which is transmitted in rat urine. The bacteria are able to survive in freshwater for about four weeks, and can infect human beings through cuts, grazes, broken skin, and the membranes of the eyes, nose and throat. The early symptoms resemble severe 'flu, so if you suffer from these shortly after working in or near water you should visit your doctor and suggest the possibility of this disease.

To reduce the risk of infection from pond or river water:
- Always keep cuts and grazes well covered and away from the water.
- Do not get the water in your mouth.
- Do not rub your eyes, nose or mouth when your hands have been in the water.
- Always wash your hands after visiting the pond, especially before eating or drinking.
- Keep a bucket of tap water nearby for hand-washing.

Glossary

biodegradable Something that can be decomposed by bacteria or other organisms.

carnivore An animal that feeds on flesh or preys on other animals; a member of the order of Carnivora.

crustacean Any member of the order Crustacea, mainly aquatic invertebrates with hard-shelled bodies such as crabs, lobsters, woodlice, etc.

decomposition The process in which organic matter is broken down into simpler substances.

detritus Materials that have been eroded or washed away, such as gravel, sand, silt, etc.

ecosystem A system of organisms occupying a habitat, together with the physical environment that they interact with.

erosion The process by which soil or land is gradually worn or washed away.

gland Any organ or cell in an animal that secretes a chemi-

cal substance (such as oils) for use by the organism.

habitat An environment naturally occupied by a particular organism. An area characterised by the set of organisms that inhabit it.

herbivore An animal that feeds on plants.

invasive Tending to intrude upon the domain of another.

invertebrate An animal with no backbone or spinal chord.

larva An insect in a state of development, often bearing little resemblance to the adult, lasting from the time it leaves the egg until its transformation into a pupa.

metamorphosis The transformation in several developmental stages that some animals undergo to become an adult, in which there is an alteration of form and habit.

mulch A mixture of wet straw, leaves, etc., spread around the roots of a plant to enrich the soil to aid its growth.

native An animal or plant found naturally in or peculiar to a country or area.

nitrate A salt of nitric acid, which can cause rapid plant growth, such as algal blooms.

non-native An animal or plant that has been introduced to a particular country or area in which it is not naturally found.

nutrient A substance that serves as or possesses nourishing qualities.

omnivore An animal that feeds on both plants and animals.

oxygenate To supply or combine with oxygen.

parasite An animal or plant that lives in or on another and draws nutrients directly from it, harming it in the process.

pH Acidity or alkalinity of a substance.

propagate Multiplying plants from shoots or layers.

pupa An insect in the developmental stage between larva and adult.

rhizome A continuously growing, usually horizontal underground stem, which puts out lateral shoots and roots at irregular intervals.

silt Fine sand, clay, or other soil carried by moving water and deposited on the bottom or on the shore of a river, stream, lake or pond.

subsoil The stratum or layer of soil lying immediately under the surface of the soil.

topsoil The surface layer of the soil.

toxin Any poisonous substance produced by microorganisms, which causes disease when present at low concentration in the body.

transpiration The loss of moisture by evaporation from the surface of a plant, especially from the leaves.

vertebrate An animal with a backbone or spinal chord.

Suppliers' addresses

SPECIALIST POND PLANT SUPPLIERS

Merton Hall Pond Ltd
Merton
Thetford
Norfolk
IP25 6QH
Tel: 01953 881763
Fax: 01953 884020
Email: mhpltd@mhp-ltd.co.uk
Web: www.mhp-ltd.co.uk

Stapeley Water Gardens Ltd
Stapeley
Nantwich
Cheshire
CW5 7LH
Tel: 01270 623868
Fax: 01270 624919
Email: stapeleywg@btinternet.com
Web: www.stapeleywatergarden.com

Wildwoods Water Gardens Ltd
Theobalds Park Road
Crews Hill
Enfield
Middlesex
EN2 9BP
Tel: 020 8366 0243
Fax: 020 8366 9892
Email: info@wildwoods.co.uk
Web: www.wildwoods.co.uk

OTHER NATIVE PLANT SUPPLIERS

British Wild Flower Plants
(Wildflowers and grasses)
31 Main Road
North Burlingham
Norwich
NR13 4TA
Tel/Fax: 01603 716 615
Email: linda@wildflowers.co.uk
Web: www.wildflowers.co.uk

Wild Flowers Nursery
(Romney Marshes as a seed source area)
62 Lower Sands
Dymchurch
Romney Marsh
Kent
TN29 0NF
Tel: 01303 873052

Yarningdale Nurseries Ltd
(Specialist wetland plant suppliers)
16 Chapel Street
Warwick
CV34 4HL
Tel: 01926 842282
Fax: 01926 842404

John Shipton
(Wildflowers and native ferns)
Y Felin
Hellan
Armgoed
Whitland
Camarthenshire
SA34 0SL
Tel: 01994 240125
Fax: 01994 241180
Email: bluebell@zoo.co.uk
Web: www.bluebellbulbs.co.uk

BIRD FOODS, FEEDERS AND NEST BOXES

Bamfords Ltd
Globe Mill
Midge Hall Lane
Midge Hall
Leyland
PR5 6TN
Tel: 01772 456300
Fax: 01772 456302
Email: sales@bamfords.co.uk
Web: www.bamfords.co.uk

CJ Wildbird Foods Ltd
The Rea
Upton Magna
Shrewbury
SY4 4UB
Tel: 0800 7312820
Fax: 01743 709504
Email: sales@birdfood.co.uk
Web: www.birdfood.co.uk

Ernest Charles & Co Ltd
Copplestone Mills
Copplestone
Crediton
Devon
EX17 5NF
Tel: 01363 84842
Fax: 01363 84147
Email: sales@ernest-charles.com
Web: www.ernest-charles.com

Jacobi Jayne & Co
Hawthorn Cottage
Maypole
Hoath
Canterbury
Kent
CT3 4LW
Tel: 01227 860388
Fax: 01227 719235
Email: enquiries@jacobijayne.com
Web: www.birdcare.com/jacobijayne

PONDS AND POND-LINERS

Bradshaws
Clifton Industrial Estate
York
Y03 8XX
Tel: 01904 691169
Fax: 01904 691133

Butyl Products
11 Radford Crescent
Billericay
Essex
CM12 0DW
Tel: 01277 653281
Fax: 01277 657921
Email: enquiries@butylproducts.co.uk
Web: www.butylproducts.co.uk

Fawcetts Tarpaulins
Linder Dept
Freepost
Back Lane
Longton
PR4 5JA
Tel: 01772 612125
Fax: 01772 615360
Email: fawcettsliners@hotmail.com
Web: www.fawcettsliners.co.uk

Midland Butyl Ltd
Windmill Hill
Biggin Lane
Nr Hulland Ward
Ashbourne
Derbyshire
DE5 3FN
Tel: 01335 372133
Fax: 01335 372199
Email: sales@midlandbutyl.co.uk
Web: www.midlandbutyl.co.uk

Monarflex
Lyon Way
Hatfield Road
St Albans
Hertfordshire
AL4 0LB
Tel: 01727 830116
Fax: 01727 868045
Email: enq@monarflex.co.uk
Web: www.monarflex.co.uk

Sussex Aquatic Services
Newhaven Road
Kingston
Lewes
East Sussex
BN7 3NE
Tel: 01273 477620
Fax: 01273 488988
Email: s.aquatics@mail.com

BENTONITE CLAY LINERS

Rawell Water Control Systems Ltd
Carr Lane, Hoylake
Merseyside
CH47 4FE
Tel: 0151 6325771
Fax: 0151 6324363
Email: postmaster@rawell.com
Web: www.rawell.com

Useful addresses

The Wildlife Trusts
The Kiln
Waterside
Mather Road
Newark NG24 1WT
Tel: 0870 0367711
Fax: 0870 0360101
Email: info@wildlife-trusts.cix.co.uk
Web: www.wildlifetrusts.org

Wildlife Watch
as for The Wildlife Trusts
Email: watch@wildlife-trusts.cix.co.uk
Web: www.wildlife-watch.org

Bat Conservation Trust
15 Cloisters House
8 Battersea Park
London SW8 4BG
Tel: 020 7627 2629
Fax: 020 7627 2628
Email: Enquiries@bats.org.uk
Web: www.bats.org.uk

British Dragonfly Society
The Haywain
Hollywater Road
Bordon
Hampshire GU35 0AD
Email: bdswebmaster@hanslope.demon.co.uk
Web: www.dragonflysoc.org.uk

British Trust for Conservation Volunteers (BTCV)
36 St Mary's Street
Wallingford
Oxfordshire OX10 0EU
Tel: 01491 839766
Fax: 01491 839646
Email: Information@btcv.org.uk
Web: www.btcv.org

British Trust for Ornithology (BTO)
The Nunnery
Thetford
Norfolk IP24 2PU
Tel: 01842 750050
Fax: 01842 750030
Email: general@bto.org
Web: www.bto.org

Butterfly Conservation Society
Manor Yard
East Lulworth
Dorset BH20 5QP
Tel: 01929 400 209
Fax: 01929 400 210
Email: info@butterfly-conservation.org
Web: www.butterfly-conservation.org

Centre for Aquatic Plant
Management (CAPM)
IACR-Long Ashton
Broadmoor Lane
Sonning
Reading
Berkshire RG4 6TH
Tel: 0118 9690072
Fax: 0118 9441730
Email: newman@aquatic.freeserve.
co.uk
Web: www.iacr.bbsrc.ac.uk/lars/
depts/cesd/geneticdgroup/
willowresearch/twatermangt.html

Field Studies Council
Preston Montford
Montford Bridge
Shrewsbury
SY4 1HW
Tel: 01743 850674
Fax: 01743 852101
Email: fsc.headoffice@
ukonline.co.uk
Web: www.field-studies-
council.org

Flora Locale
36 Kingfisher Court
Hambridge Road
Newbury
RG14 5SJ
Tel: 01635 550380
Fax: 01635 550230
Email: floralocale@
naturebureau.co.uk
Web: www.floralocale.org

Froglife
Mansion House
27 -28 Market Place
Halesworth
Suffolk
IP19 9AY
Tel: 01986 873733
Fax: 01986 874744
Email: froglife@froglife.org
Web: www.froglife.org

Henry Doubleday Research
Association (HDRA)
Ryton Organic Gardens
Ryton on Dunsmore
Coventry
CV8 3LG
Tel: 02476 303517
Fax: 02476 639229
Email: enquiry@hdra.org.uk
Web: www.hdra.org.uk

Herpetological Conservation Trust
655a Christchurch Toad
Boascombe
Bournemouth
Dorset
BH1 4AP
Tel: 01202 391319
Fax: 01202 392785
Email: HerpConsTrust@hcontrst.
force9.net
Web: www.hcontrst.f9.co.uk

Landlife
National Wildflower Centre
Court Hey Park
Liverpool
L16 3NA
Tel: 0151 7371819
Fax: 0151 7371820
Email: info@landlife.org.uk
Web: www.landlife.org.uk

Plantlife
21 Elizabeth Street
London
SW1W 9RP
Tel: 020 7808 0100
Fax: 020 7730 8377
Email: enquiries@plantlife.org.uk
Web: www.plantlife.org

Pond Conservation Trust
C/O Oxford Brookes University
Gipsy Lane
Headington
Oxford
OX3 0BP
Tel: 01865 483249
Fax: 01865 483282
Web: www.pondtrust.org.uk

Royal Society for the Protection
of Birds (RSPB)
The Lodge
Sandy
Bedfordshire
SG19 2DL
Tel: 01767 680551
Fax: 01767 692365
Email: bird@rspb.demon.co.uk
Web: www.rspb.org.uk

Water Garden
(Open garden 4 days a week (Fri,
Sat, Sun, Mon), 2-6pm, April-
September only)
High Croft
Morrend
Wembworthy
Chumleigh
Devon
EX18 7SG
Tel: 01837 83566

STATUTORY CONSERVATION
AGENCIES

In England
English Nature (EN)
Northminster House
Peterborough
PE1 1UA
Tel: 01733 455100
Fax: 01733 455103
Email: enquiries@english-
nature.org.uk
Web: www.english-nature.org.uk

In Northern Ireland
Environmental Heritage Services
(EHS)
Environmental Protection
Calvert House
23 Castle Place
Belfast
Northern Ireland
BT1 1FY
Tel: 02890 251477
Tel: 02890 254754 (Water Quality
Unit)
Fax: 02890 254700
Email: ehsinfo@doeni.gov.uk
Web: www.ehni.gov.uk

In Scotland
Scottish Natural Heritage (SNH)
12 Hope Terrace
Edinburgh
EH9 2AS
Tel: 0131 4474784
Fax: 0131 4462277
Email: enquiries@snh.gov.uk
Web: www.snh.org.uk

In UK
Joint Nature Conservation
Committee (JNCC)
Monkstone House
City Road
Peterborough
PE1 1JY
Tel: 01733 562626
Fax: 01733 555948
Web: www.jncc.gov.uk

In Wales
Countryside Council for Wales
(CCW)
Plas Penrhos
Fford Penrhos
Bangor
Gwynedd
LL57 2LQ
Tel: 01248 385000
Fax: 01248 355782
Email: hq_reception@ccw.gov.uk
Web: www.ccw.gov.uk

STATUTORY ENVIRONMENTAL
REGULATORS

In England and Wales
Environment Agency (EA)
Rio House
Waterside Drive
Aztec Wesst
Almondsbury
Bristol
BS12 4UD
Tel: 01454 624400
Fax: 01454 624409
Email: enquiries@environment-
agency.gov.uk
Web: www.environment-
agency.gov.uk

In Northern Ireland
Environmental Heritage Services
(EHS)
Water Quality Unit
Calvert House
23 Castle Place
Belfast
Northern Ireland
BT1 1FY
Tel: 02890 254754
Fax: 02890 254700
Email: ehsinfo@doeni.gov.uk
Web: www.ehni.gov.uk

In Scotland
Scottish Environmental Protection
Agency (SEPA)
Head Quarters
Erskine Court
The Castle Business Park
Stirling
Scotland
FK9 4TR
Tel: 01786 457700
Fax: 01786 446885
Email: info@sepa.org.uk
Web: www.sepa.org.uk

Further Reading

Baker, Nick
Nick Baker's Bug Book
New Holland Publishers, 2002
ISBN 1 85974 895 3

Baines, Chris
How to Make a Wildlife Garden
Frances Lincoln, 2000
ISBN 0 71121 711 4

Beddard, Roy
The Garden Bird Year
New Holland Publishers, 2001
ISBN 1 85974 655 1

Beebee, Trevor
Pond Life
Whittet Books, 1995
ISBN 0 90548 399 5

Bennett, Jackie
The Wildlife Garden Month-by-Month
David & Charles, 1997
ISBN 0 71530 573 5

Chanin, Paul
The Natural History of Otters
Facts on File Inc., 1986
ISBN 0 81601 288 1

Chinery, Michael
Butterflies of Britain and Europe
Collins and The Wildlife Trusts, 1998
ISBN 0 00220 059 7

Chinery, Michael
A Field Guide to the Insects of Britain and Northern Europe
HarperCollins, 1993
ISBN 0 00219 918 1

Chinery, Michael
Garden Creepy Crawlies
Whittet Books, 1998
ISBN 1 87358 041 X

Croft, P.S.
A Key to the Major Groups of British Freshwater Invertebrates
Field Studies Council, Vol 6, No 3. 1986
ISBN 1 85153 181 6

De'ath, Jane and Heaton, Anne
Freshwater
Richmond Publishing Co. Ltd and The Wildlife Trusts, 2000
ISBN 1 86989 201 1

De Feu, Chris
Nestboxes
British Trust for Ornithology, 1993
ISBN 0 90379 329 6

Friday, L.E.
A Key to the Adults of British Water Beetles
Backhuy Publishers, Field Studies Council, Vol. 7, No 1, 1988
ISBN 1 85153 189 0

Gibbons, B.
Field Guide to the Insects of Britain and Northern Europe
The Crowood Press, 1996
ISBN 1 85223 895 X

Golley, Mark
The Complete Garden Bird Book
New Holland Publishers, 2001
ISBN 1 84330 035 4

Hammond, Nicholas (Series Editor)
The Wildlife Trusts Guide to Butterflies and Moths
New Holland Publishers, 2002
ISBN 1 85974 959 3

Hammond, Nicholas (Series Editor)
The Wildlife Trusts Guide to Garden Wildlife
New Holland Publishers, 2002
ISBN 1 85974 961 5

Hammond, Nicholas (Series Editor)
The Wildlife Trusts Guide to Insects
New Holland Publishers, 2002
ISBN 1 85974 962 3

Hammond, Nicholas (Series Editor)
The Wildlife Trusts Handbook of Garden Wildlife
New Holland Publishers, 2002
ISBN 1 85974 960 7

Hill, Fran
Wildlife Gardening – A Practical Handbook
Derbyshire Wildlife Trust, 1998
ISBN 1 87144 400 4

Matthews, Nigel
Garden for Birds
School Garden Co.,
ISBN 1 85116 805 2

Moss, Stephen and Cottridge, David
Attracting Birds to your Garden
New Holland Publishers, 2000
ISBN 1 85974 005 7

Oddie, Bill
Bill Oddie's Birds of Britain and Ireland
New Holland Publishers, 1998
1 85368 898 3

Olsen, Lars-Henrik, Sunesen, Jakob and Pedersen, Bente Vita
Small Freshwater Creatures
Oxford University Press, 2001
ISBN 0 19850 797 6

Oxford, R.
Minibeast Magic – Kind-hearted Capture Techniques for Invertebrates
A Yorkshire Wildlife Trust Publication, 1999
ISBN 9 780950 946020

Packham, Chris
Chris Packham's Back Garden Nature Reserve
New Holland Publishers, 2001
ISBN 1 85974 520 2

Papworth, David
A Fishkeeper's Guide to Garden Ponds
Salamander Books, 1997
ISBN 0 86101 129 5

Powell, Dan
A Guide to the Dragonflies of Great Britain
Arlequin Press, 1999
ISBN 1 90015 905 8

Rackham, Oliver
The History of the Countryside
J.M. Dent & Sons Ltd, 1986
ISBN 0 460 86091 7

Strachan, Rob
Water Voles
Whittet Books Ltd, 1997
ISBN 1 87358 033 9

Thompson, Shirley
Bats in the Garden
School Garden Co.,
ISBN 1 85116 803 6

Thurman, Peter
Plants for the Water Garden
Tiger Books, 1994
ISBN 1 85501 992 2

Williams P. et al
The Pond Book – A Guide to the Management and Creation of Ponds
Ponds Conservation Trust, Oxford, 1999

Dig a Pond for Dragonflies
British Dragonfly Society
(available from Mrs J. Silsby
1 Haydn Avenue
Purley
Surrey GR8 4AG

Index

Page numbers in **bold** refer to illustrations in the text

ACKNOWLEDGEMENTS

I would like to thank all the people at New Holland, especially Lorna Sharrock for all her help and understanding during a somewhat turbulent time. I would also like to thank the staff of Wiltshire Wildlife Trust for their help and advice, in particular P.D. who is a walking encyclopaedia of wildlife. I have used information gathered in my research work and travels, none of which would have happened if it weren't for the support, kindness and friendship of Trevor Beebee and Maggie. Finally, I would like to thank my parents and friends, especially George and Jez for just being there!

Louise Bardsley

Photographic acknowledgements
All photographs by David M. Cottridge, with the exception of the following:
John Bailey: pp10, 15, 19, 31
Nature Photographers Ltd: Hugh Clark: p69; Geoff Du Feu: p7; Chris Grey-Wilson: pp43(t), 71; Jean Hall: p44(b);
Paul Sterry: pp40, 44(t), 46, 72(tr)
PA News: p6
Richard Revels: pp1, 4(3rd vignette, b), 5, 13(t), 14, 18, 34, 37, 47, 48, 50, 54, 56, 58, 63, 70, 72(br)
Peter Stiles: front cover, p20
Will Watson: p29
Alan Williams: pp4(l), 17, 12, 68
Windrush Photos: Hugh Clark: p41; Mark Lucas: p33; David Tomlinson: p66(b)
Photo of pond-liners on p21: with thanks to Wildwoods Water Gardens Ltd., www.wildwoods.co.uk

Artwork acknowledgements
All artwork by Wildlife Art Ltd, with the exception of the following:
David Daly: pp3, 14, 36, 37, 42, 67

(t= top; b=bottom; c=centre; l=left; r=right)